MINUTES
Within An
HOURGLASS

Nothing is Reach!
Beyond My Reach.
I am Upward Bound

Salisha D Hill

Upward Bound Graduate
2011

MINUTES
Within An
HOURGLASS

SALISHA D. HILL

authorHOUSE®

AuthorHouse™
1663 Liberty Drive
Bloomington, IN 47403
www.authorhouse.com
Phone: 1-800-839-8640

Published by AuthorHouse   01/21/2013

ISBN: 978-1-4772-9500-7 (sc)
ISBN: 978-1-4772-9498-7 (hc)
ISBN: 978-1-4772-9499-4 (e)

Library of Congress Control Number: 2012922600

Any people depicted in stock imagery provided by Thinkstock are models, and such images are being used for illustrative purposes only.
Certain stock imagery © Thinkstock.

This book is printed on acid-free paper.

Dedicated to my loving fiancé, Daultin, and
to my family who has been there for me through everything,
including my twin sister, Saleena, who helped me edit this book.
Also, to those who have played a role in getting me
to where I am today. Lastly, to those who have been angels
and guardians in my life and the lives of others.

Contents

A Fairytale Truth

I'll be a Sleeping Beauty without her kiss
Aladdin without his last wish
I'll be a Cinderella without her slipper
Belle without her beast
I'll be Snow White without her dwarves
Ariel without her way to shore
I'll be Dora without Boots
Blue without clues
Tom Thumb shrunk to nothing
The princess with a million peas
Rapunzel with cancer
Ballerina without her dancer
A magician with no tricks
A doctor who's too sick
A judge who is biased
A person who is priced
A singer with no talent
A scale with no balance
Without you, I'm nothing I'm supposed to be
I'm a lost child, I'm a small child
A concrete floor that is supposed to be tiled
I'll be a radio with no sound
A TV with no signal
This was never love, but it was better
I hope this won't be my last letter
Without you I'm nothing I'm supposed to be
I'm a cup with a hole at the bottom
I'm a fairy tale without a happy ending
I'm a race of people without a language
The shoulder you leaned on is now weak
The help you so often needed, you seeked
When you were hungry, dinner was ready
A fine young gentleman who needed to be steady
Without you, I'm nothing I'm supposed to be
My mind goes blank, I can't think

My eyes blue, tear-filled, I can't blink
My heart is torn open, sewn shut, will shrink
I'll be Peter Pan without Tink
Harry Potter without his friends
This is where it's pressured, rules tend to bend
Thoughts begin to wander into a pretty, black hole
Then every Christmas you know you'll get coal
Every breath you take breaks until you're very cold
Your words slip out, you don't mean what you say
You seek help from the One who'll listen, you pray
You say, "I've lost someone dear, I'll miss her year to year, I've lost all my
friends, my peers,
I'm nothing I'm supposed to be, so on sheds my tears."

A Little Girl

A little girl, about ten years old
Couldn't tell what should have been told
She cried each night, alone and helpless
Who could help her, who could save her?

If she told, what would happen?
Would no one believe her, would she get hurt again?
Where would she go? A new place? The same? Homeless?
Again she cried, alone and helpless

A little girl, about twelve years old
Finally told what she knew she should tell
Even though her pain was so cold
She knew her life would no longer be hell

When she told, it was a shock to all
The man kicked out and hated
No longer would she have to give herself away
She could keep to herself, alone

A little girl who got abused
A little girl who got used
A little girl who hated life
A little girl who told her strife

A Mother's Love

Have you ever wondered when you're home and alone
How you've shined a light that has so brightly shown
We know how much your heart fits us like a glove
When the most powerful fit is a mother's love

A Single White Rose

he gave me
one
white
rose
he didn't give me anything special, just
one, single
crème, white
rose
he wasn't mean nor nice nor ugly nor cute or
in need of an apology or with the need to say sorry
but he still gave me
only one single
velvety-smooth crème white
rose
where would I put
only one single solitary, individual
velvety-smooth, beautiful crème white
rose
on a table? a desk? a counter? a shelf?
a windowsill, of course!
perfect for
only one single solitary individual lonesome
velvety-smooth beautiful lovely captivating crème white
rose
I placed it on a windowsill
by my front door
where the sun shown everyday
I put this
only one single solitary individual lonesome
velvety-smooth beautiful lonely captivating crème white
rose
next to the thing that could keep it alive

the sun
it teased each petal, each leaf, each thorn
it seeked the happiness of each thorn, each leaf, each petal
just like he did when he handed me
one
white
rose
just like I did when I took
only one single solitary individual lonesome
velvety-smooth beautiful lovely captivating crème white
rose
from his hand
only
one
white rose

Above

I was sitting under a dark sky
Naming the stars and clouds
I felt your warm and clammy hands
But I realized all the sky would fall down

The bright white snowflakes of winter
The cold rain of spring
The bitter rays of heat of summer
The golden leaves of autumn
All fall, all will fall

I was sitting under a dark sky
Naming the stars and clouds
I felt your comforting hands on my waists
But I realized all the sky would fall down
And yet I didn't care

After I Moved

This is what I see when I open my eyes
I have everything I can dream of
But when I close them, I come to realize
The only thing my heart desires is gone

All the Possibilities

Romania awaits, I'm on the outskirts of time
Invisible creations vividly displayed in my mind
Outward expansion of my mind into words
All these things we don't expect I want to occur

Jumping off of airplanes, hiding in the woods
People who really aren't sure are surely reassured

A child in the arms of a dying mother
A newborn in the arms of little brother
A kid not wanted with a family to adopt her
I want to help each of them out
That's what my life will be all about

One thing I want to do most in my life
Is just be me until the day I die
And that'll always be who I am even after thirty-five

As I drive my Jeep down country roads
And as I pay my way with maps
I'll help people through their struggles
I'll help them unlock their traps

I've let go of nothing
I've said goodbye not at all
I've simply let my memory fade
As I wait for the world to fall

Alternate Universe

The passion, the fear, the longing
Together
Everything's different
Everything's weird
A world I'm not used to
A world in which
I'm alive
Where you are there
When I wake up
And as I close my eyes at night
Always returning
Even when I doubt the truth
Even when your love is clear
I'm left returning to the point
I'm clueless about this all

Always Me

I am hidden now
You can't see me through this dark mask
But I'm still myself

Asphyxiated Heart: An Elegy of Me

My heart beats for only me, thump, thump, thump
My heart beats only because of you, thump, thump, thump
Soft pounds of unrequited words, love
My heart beats slow upon gasps of release
Gasps of breath getting harder to take
My heart you caused to choke upon fatal dedication
Deadly contemplation from words unsaid
Not admitted to earnest souls nor worlds unknown
Since you're gone I suffer simple suffocation
The results of a twisted asphyxiation
Dying under the presence of 'no you'
You've brought me here as I choke and die
To this place I don't want to be
Nothing can lift me from the place I'm in now
My heart beats for only me, thump, thump
My heart beats only because of you
You're gone, thump, thump, thud, stop
Twisted asphyxiation, simple suffocation
Deadly contemplation, fatal dedication
Thump, thump, thud, stop. Why?

Autoimmune Disease Devastation

As I have lived
And as you have lived with me
You have been the center
Of my existence
My world
My love

And not a day goes by
Where I don't love you
Where I don't care
Where I don't think about you
Or worry

But I have seen the weakness
I have seen the haste
Of this disease
That has taken hold of you
Slowly killing you each day

So devastating death can be
When you see it at the doorstep
Of a friend
At the doorstep of the one
Who knew you better than anyone

And hope isn't so easy to regain
When so many have been lost before
It's hard to believe you'll make it through
When I have witnessed death take over
Sick loved ones before

And I know your strength will be
The thing that continues to revive you
Because not a day will go by
Where I'll be willing to let you go
Always in my heart, my love
The one who knew me most

Awaiting Escape

who will be willing to pick me up
not be scared of wounding me further
the only evidence of deliverance

what will I give to be able to see him
have myself wrapped in his arms
the only escape of reality

when will all this cease to exist
find out what really needs to happen
the only elixir of pain

where will I end up in the end
belonging, not, happy, not, here, home
the only eviction of death

why have I felt like this for so long
going down deeper, further
the only essence of depression

how would things be different if I stayed
living each day with a reason
the only excuse of sanity

Beer Can in the Driver's Seat

Horns loud
Headlights bright
Metal meets metal
Crash tonight

I scream, he screams
We scream loud
Pain envelops
Death lingers around us now

People whisper, worried sick
Wondering what happened
Wondering who'll live

Begging

I'm sitting here, just not sure who's going to
Hold out a hand to help me or
Push me back down to the ground
All I'm sure of is that I'm scared and
That the fruit of the world is rotting

I'm lying here, wanting the light to shine
But these clouds are thick and
The gravity weighs them down onto me
And I'm sure I need help but
I'm afraid to lose all my friends if I tell

I'm dying here, longing for hope
Depression is an understatement but
I'm sure no one is to understand that
Sadness is my embarrassment, so I hide it
So I'm calling out, high tonight, please save me

I'm fading away, out of my closing reality
Losing all control and I need to steady myself
If I'm determined to live through this
Everything that means the most to me
Was taken at no one's cost and at all's loss

I'm reaching out, asking for help
Begging for release of this hole
Not just sadness, but stress and hopelessness, lost
And there may be no reason for it, it just is
It is what it is, but I need to ask
Please help me, save me, please

Believe

It kills me inside everyday
When I wake up
And it's not your face I see
And I have no reason to believe
No reason to try to go on

Living so sadly without you
Walking without purpose
Crying for you, screaming too
I want you so badly, please come back
Don't leave me hanging like this

I won't give up on you though
No matter how much you don't care
Cuz you were there for me
In my time of need
In my head talking, shh, shh

The world will go on as it does
And the people will go on
But I will be here
Just not letting go of this cliff, my life
I will believe for him
My world

Biggest Mistake

No matter how hard I try
It's never good enough
One note written seven times
And I'm left empty-handed, what the fuck

You're my instant message bad boy
While I'm waiting for a reply
I type out poems silently
While you're probably getting high

And I don't know why I always like the guys
Who always seem so bad
Because one day I'll wonder why
I always feel this sad

Liking you was my biggest mistake
And love seems like a lie
I don't know if love is fake
But it seems to be the hardest goodbye

So this is my official way
Of letting this pain go
And even though I liked you yesterday
I wanted to let you know
I won't like you anymore, not even today
And definitely not tomorrow

Blam

Why is blam such a small word,
Describing such huge destruction?
When something is about to explode,
You'd better use instruction.

Why is the airplane upside down,
When they're usually faced upward?
And why is it on the ground,
When they're usually in the sky?

Blue Lips

Tell me what you love so much about my simple kisses
Tell me why you love the lasting hatred
Tell me why you desire connection with my red lips
I thought your favorite color was blue
Carefully place me in your arms
I'm still very unconscious
Carefully remove my clothes
This drug won't wear off fast enough
Some call this rape
But you know my unconsciousness wants it

So you don't expect me to wake up
Weary and aware and only in my underwear
You freak out but I kiss you back
But when you pull away from me, you leave me no choice
I grab your hair and take control

Tell me what you love so much about my simple kisses
Tell me why you dread connection with my dead lips
Especially when IT'S YOUR FAULT
You held me and unclothed me
I wake up and see that, now you can't do what you wanted
You can't rape me, you're so weak, you even had to drug me
I may be smart, maybe pretty
But I will not be taken advantage of
You will love me or hate me, you chose love

So when I wake up, now it's you that's dead
Cuz you can't handle the outcome of your mistakes
The only decision you made was rape
So I let it slide this one time, but you freak out, you're afraid
When I kiss back, you can't decide what you like
So that's why I had to bury your love tonight
Because you knew I loved you too
That's why it's now your lips that are blue

Blue Memories

Open my eyes slowly
Remember I can't
Remember I won't
My dream was like heaven
Remember I don't

His midnight blue eyes, his ice blue heart
His blue depression, his blue me
But our love as well as sadness
Was unique

Pillow on the floor, him not next to me
Me alone with emptiness and sheets
Get off the bed, put a gun to my head
A lifetime of regrets released
A trigger's relief
Damn jam, why now when I know I can

Giving up on ending
Because I remember I can't
Remember I won't
My nightmare's a reality
Remember I don't

Body of Mourning

I'm standing among straight lines of fresh graveyard dirt
You're the body of mourning whose heart will not work
The one of whose heart wholly deserved
To beat
I'm lying among the starts of darkening eternity
My hair against grass surrounding the tall trees
Leaves around my body weak
Are also on his grave
I'm drowning amidst the crying flames of rain
Weaker and weaker, your death has made
Me and everyone, our lives will fade
Lost and forgotten
I'm dying inside myself; I'm a body of mourning
Memories are lost in REM dreams
Can't let go of your heart, the rain, defeat
When your heart was the one who ceased to beat

Breaking the Bones

My heart which is torn from my chest
My thoughts to sadness, I admit how I've transgressed
The days of old, I miss the most
The days of now, I don't dare to imagine
My thoughts bring your smile, the only thing I see of you now
I see how you made me smile, inside out
I see how you made me love, upside down
I love what you had, your loud discrepancies
I love who you were when I could see
You for you, me for me, the world was mine
My dreams of life, of you, of me
The time alone though tears the pages
Out of a once happy life
Jealous of my own past
Breaking the bones, grown to last, turned to glass
Breaking the bones, turned old and grown

Broken Figure

You stare at yourself for minutes at a time
The mirror tired of looking at your broken figure
The bruises left behind from past attacks
The missing half of your heart
He still has
The scars just appearing
The scabs slowly disappearing
The scratches only healing
The pain is all your feeling
Nothing stops the reflection you crave
The mirror is sick of seeing your broken figure
The swelling is not enough
The pain, the hurt, all this suffering
Aching, sore heart
The life that's been torn apart
To pieces, to nothing
This broken figure walking dark hallways
Along bridgeless waters
Alone, by yourself, broken
Someone, who is no one, by yourself
Broken figure

Broken Hearted

It's amazing how we grew up so fast
From classmates to friends that would last
It's so beautiful how we became so close
From a budding seed to a small delicate rose
It's so perfect the Lord's deed is to allow this
Creating a bond so strong, but also creating risk
One day we were sure of everything, so sure of it all
The next I was packing to leave, our friendship would fall
It's sad how our relationship would cease to exist
From friends for life to people we miss
It's so unnecessary the feelings I feel now
From a ready laugh to automatic frown
It's so wrong the Lord's deed is to allow this
Not only creating risk, but putting it into action
And now since our ways have parted
I want to say
It's no fun being brokenhearted

Came and Gone

There was rain that day
And you had disappeared
I had no clue where you were
But I knew you weren't near

Sometimes I see your face
And I long to touch it
Sometimes I hear your voice
And my face lit

But a part of me realizes
You didn't just leave
You took everything with you
Everything except me

And now it's raining
And I see your face
And I don't want to leave
But I slowly walk away from the chase
I go away for now
I'll wait another day

Can You Ever Be

Can you ever be in love with someone who doesn't love you back
You think you're in the right direction
But you've started on the wrong tracks
You feel so alone in whatever you do
You know where you live is not home
You know you're stuck behind the moon
Because everywhere you are the sun's not shone
No matter how hard you even try to succeed
You're always a hundred steps behind
No matter how hard you try to stay the lead
You're the one they keep playing on rewind

Christmas Love

What I like about Christmas is
All the experiences and the times we miss
The special Christmas dinner food
To get in the wonderful Christmas mood
To open the presents around the tree
The things that mean a lot to me
When all the gifts are open and torn
Is the day Jesus Christ was born

Clockwork

Days are fading by and by, time to say goodbye
Hours slipping from it, glass gone
Time goes slow upon unknown
Mysteries remain unsolved in hearts of gold
Life goes missing as life grows old
Minds remembrance and hearts memories

Country Life

A farmer cutting wheat or a bird in the sky
Tell me which one you'd be and then tell me why
The farmer barely paid enough and strives to get his food
While the bird is gliding in the sky wishing he could, too
When the sun is burning on the farmer's back
The birds are quietly gazing at their painful pasts
The farmers whipping bulls to get along the path
I hope a bird wasn't under a wheel
That'd be awfully sad

Crying, Not Sleeping

I miss them all, my friends
I miss him so much, my love
I miss my life, myself
And now I cry alone, suffer

I cannot let them go, they are my everything
I cannot let go of him, he is my life
I cannot let go of this sadness, it keeps me alive
Waiting each breath like my last

I cry so much, each tear so powerful
Rock myself asleep, to my safety, or to my hell
How invisible the pain is, but so plain to see
That each and every one was a part of me

At night, I hold him close
Cuz no one can see
The tears, the power, the loss
And no one hears me

Sometimes, I stay awake all night and think
His hair, his eyes, his smile, gone
Or I think of what I lost
Dwelling on lost times of happiness, control

I try to get past my living nightmares
But I can't, they suffice my life, enough
I lived for what I am missing now
And hope that will get me past somehow

Daddy's Home

Daddy's home again
Drunk
Throwing down his briefcase and jacket
Shoes and hat
Keys
Yelling, must've had a bad day
Tell me about it
He seems so sad and tired
Wrinkles around his eyes seem
More pronounced
Revealing his age, his aging
His voice is shaking
Work is hard
It must've been harder
But still he's drunk
And still he's drinking

So down on my knees, I begin praying
"Dear Lord, Dear Lord, Dear Heavenly Father"
Please help me, please help my father
Drinking and driving, screaming and crying
I don't want my life to end this way
I don't want our lives to fade away
Even the emptiness becomes my friend at times like these
Even loneliness walks me through
His problems, our problems, my problems
So, please help me, please help my father
Please Dear Lord, please Holy Father"

Daddy didn't come home
Daddy was drunk
He threw on the breaks
Slammed, swerved, splashed, and sunk
Now I cry silently
As I looked in his casket
Solemnly, lonely, dead
Wrinkles apparent, weaknesses of a parent

I get down on my knees and pray
"Dear Lord, Dear Lord, Dear Heavenly Father
Please save me, please save my father
He was drinking and driving
Now I'm screaming and crying
And now my father has gone home
Amen."

Darkest in Daylight

In the afternoon wind
When everything was freer, fuller
We, me and you
Embraced that hope
If only a little
We embraced it
And under the dark universe
Covered by blue skies
We pretended together
That everything was alright
As long as it was you and me together
I was fine
And I hoped like hell you were too
But in the end
Truth was the thing to destroy
Life, my will to live
My house home emptied
My friend home dead
And now in the afternoon wind
Under the dark universe
I've got nothing left

Days Left

I walked beside your hospital bed
No voice to talk, plenty to be said
Cancer hard to battle, every will to heal
The family alive, upset by this ordeal
I'm sorry you have to go through this
The nurses try, but it's getting harder to live
I cried going in, on the inside
I cried being there, I held it in
I cried as I left, I let it all out
Because I know there's no doubt
You only have days left until you have to say goodbye
I hope, dear Lord, it won't be tonight

Days Pass

Days pass like chapters in a book
One you can't put down
One you can't stop reading
One that never ends
And days pass like a spring rain
Fade and return, giving life
Fade and return, bringing destruction
Fade and return, dragging me underneath
And days pass, mortifying me
Catching me in bad times
Tripping me in good times
And watching me the whole time, laughing, mocking
Days pass by me briskly, briefly, bravely
And I'm running, catching, but never actually succeeding
Yet I'm just sitting here waiting, betraying myself
Yet I'm drifting away, from the days
Reality only slowly setting in, but always changing
Renewing itself in different ways
And I'm running to catch it, falling for the trap
Finding sanctuary in this sedentary place
A world lost in itself, its many cultures
Lost in time as days pass

Death of Caesar

Growing tension, conspiracy
Firing up hatred, intensity
Take the knife, hide it slow
Walk up fast, on death row
Secret desire, eliminate the power
When it happens, blood shower
Now we're here, March fifteenth
It's about to happen, beauty
Plunge it in, pull it out
Kill him slow, but kill him now
History made, people run
Cries aloud, "The job is done!"

Defeat

Angels are bright still
Though the brightest fell
The brightest couldn't be the best
So he was sent to hell

Angel of light
Beauty and power
Thirsty for God's place
Greedy to be higher

Gathered a group
A third of the heavens
Rebelled against Jesus
He had no chance then

After the battle
So many weary and tired
A third of the heavens banished
To hell they retired

Lucifer of light
Hell of darkness
Ironic how the meaning of light
Now resides in the darkness

Earthly Endeavors

Dark black trees, scarlet red sky
The rain comes pouring like the tears in my eyes
My pain feels like lightning, it's stricken me down
My cries are like thunder, I hear all around
The rain is filling the river, my feelings overflowed
People see the flood, but they go around, even after
All the things I've showed
The clouds clear up, maybe there's still hope
The sky darkens up, the earth shakes then
The rain pours, tears falling, peace breaks
I silence, then turn around
Right before my nightmares shove me down
He locks the door and I'm silent, not a sound
I can't let anyone know I hate it
Yet, I can't stand putting up with this
They all hear my heart break
The sound of my soul shake
He leaves the room, he got what he want
His voice, my breath, these sounds will haunt
I scream inside my biggest pillow
The anger let out like a big volcano
The lava comes out, runs down
The side of a volcano, lived a town
But nothing is there anymore
The pain escaped
A bunch of new people showed
The memories poured out like the rain sometimes does
The rain never cleared, clouds are alive
The pain and this anger escape forever
But at least there will never be a we
Never

Empty Questions

Blue lips, white skin
Death's apparent
Wide eyes, sparkleless
Life's barren

Finger twitch, muscle spasm
Soul-less body
Breathing, heartbeat
Nothing here, Godly

Police come, siren's on
Broken bones, body bag
Life, murder
Suicide
I beg of you, please don't cry
My life question was always why

Why did he kill me?
Why not himself?
Why can't I say goodbye?
Why can't I answer these myself?

Because I'm dead.

Extremes

I'm standing in the rain that just began pouring
And this disaster I'm in the middle of
Causes death, destruction, and mourning

And as the earth falls down all around me
There's you
And as I slip into this unforgiving coma
I see you

Mud slides and ocean currents
Are the way I feel
I'm sliding quickly down a mountain burning
But suddenly I'm speeding up, drowning

I'm standing in the rain that just began pouring
And the lightning and thunder that knock me down
Gives you the strength to pull me from my mourning

And as the world burns and crumbles beneath my fingertips
There's you
And as I slowly die underneath it all
I see you

Hectic happenings and deep despair
Are the way I feel
I'm finding things to do so fast
Then the pain comes, feels so real

I can't win in this world of disaster
I can't win with myself
You balance out every emotion I have
Whether I'm in heaven or hell

Eye of the Beholder

Beauty is one, above any, above all
Brains of today, tomorrow will fall
The minds of once children
The minds of once will crawl
On the floors, beaten down
Never taught strength, always frown
Tired of days, once were long
Ready of the future, all strong
Bonds build, love fails, beauty betrayal
Brains of today shall learn of tomorrow

Eye of Ghetto Prisoners

Fake smiles
Hidden cries

Prayers said
Soon goodbyes

Forgotten shelter
Unsure eyes

Ignorance in mourning among the wise

Falling Out of Reach

These tests are slowly pulling me away
Controlling my thoughts and life and pain
Blinding the hope, the truth, the you
Turning peace of white to night of blue
Tripping over fallen mistakes, goals
Tears falling, all that remains shows
I try to hold your heart in the palm of my hand
But the time allows it to turn to sand

Fly Away Kiss

Thoughtless whispers, longing eyes
My heart for you, I won't deny
Timeless wonders, lengthy days
But, you know, it's for you I pray
Say goodbye, fly away kiss
Blow it to me, I'll hold it like this
Tell me words I long to hear
You're special, I love you, dear

Freedom

I wish to be let out of war
To be the last to set foot in it
To be the first to feel brave
I wish to be let out of war

I wish to be released
Out of side taking
Out of that cage
I wish to be released

I wish to set peace with Britain
To tell them how we feel
To teach their children differently
Instead of war and guilt

I wish American's will listen
To what they have to say
What will happen if they don't accept or apologize

Game Plan

The true end of tragedy is to purify the passions
When you can live with what you love, you'll learn life is livable

What's right is what's left if you do everything else wrong
Do the best with what you have because that's the best you can do

There is no coming to consciousness without pain
Knowing everyday repeats itself is tough to swallow and harder to accept
as each day passes

All sin tends to be addictive and the terminal point of addiction is what
is called damnation
You know what you do is wrong, but you do it anyway because you don't
know any other way

Things turn out best for those who make the best of the way things turn out
So use the sour lemons and the sweet sugar to make something milder

Don't let someone be a priority in your life when you are still an option
in their life
It will only break your heart, not theirs

A real act of honesty is not enough to be honored by everyone, but being
witnessed by you and God alone
And you only have to be true to yourself to learn how to be true to
others and it only matters what God sees

Never take a person's dignity; it is worth everything to them and
nothing to you
It will only reveal to them that you are just as fragile and human as they are

Until one has loved an animal, part of their soul remains unawakened
You love a pet more because they understand and keep their mouths shut.
Sometimes that's the best advice.

Better to fail with honor than succeed with fraud
Because you will be faced with the fraud eventually

Get Up and Start Something

There's nothing to do, I'm killing time
There is no job, not making a dime
I can't do nothing, you're locking the cage
Everyone's gone, you've filled me with rage
The baby is crying, we've ran out of food
The dog is barking at whose to intrude
Mom's screaming about 'not enough time'
Her boyfriend is leaving, blamed her on lying
I'm stuck in a place, rough to live life
I can't wait til some new years arrive
To move out, go to college, start a life

God

Lying on my back, face towards the sky
Looking at the clouds, wishing I was that high
The sky moves very slowly, but time flies by
I wish I could stop time to figure out why

Each day I wake up and in God I believe
Because I know He will not go and deceive
My feelings fly by, but I know He still loves me
My feelings fly by, but through Him help is received

But other times I feel bad and lose faith
Even though He guides my footsteps every day
I listen to my Father in every single way
And I won't let temptation control what I say

Going, Going, Gone

Forever I'm leaving, never to be seen again
I'll be followed by my choices, until the end
Leave me to silence, I'll never say a word
I'm flying away from here, I'll never be heard

My bag beside me, I'm going today
I'm sorry, darling, this is the only way
I've brought along bare minimum
A suitcase, a jacket, a passport, and gum

Inside my suitcase, I've brought along my needs
I have a Bible, clothes, a book to read
A map, some pictures, and most of all
A camera to capture moments that call

Not much do I think about the future or past
All that matters is the present, now will pass
And as I'll never understand what I did
Just know I'll never return, today is sold to the highest bid

Grow Up

Why don't you visit
Why don't you call
Why don't you listen
Why don't you talk

When will you understand
When will you care
When will you be a man
When will you dare

Who do you think you are
Bossing me around
Why do you think you're so hard
Pushing me down

Even though I like you for who you may be
I'd like for you to be mine, do you love me maybe

Had to Go

I never wanted to leave, I never wanted to go
I always needed you to try to help me grow
Everything I loved is gone, even you
And when you said you loved me, I should have too
My mistakes are getting worse
I'm buried under this threatening curse
My heart is with you, torn in two
And now my emptiness hurts

Help Me Understand

The days are growing fast
Soon the world will be past
I can't imagine what it's like
To live a life and then die
I feel sorry because the mystery
I don't know if heaven is trickery
I ask the Lord for guidance
And, in return, live my life
To the fullest

His Control

How high do I have to reach
To feel Your power within me
To raise my hand in the sky
And feel Your breath on my cheek
To hide behind a tower
And feel as mighty as the world
Yet open myself to the Lord
And feel as tiny as this little girl

Home

Home is where the heart is
That's with you
I'm head over heels
That's what love can do

Simple kisses in the rain
Midnight dates make you insane
You get dizzy, your heart starts to beat
And all around your body, you feel heat

Everything spinning in your head
When you kiss, when you touch
But when things won't stop
You get scared, but you fly up above

It's amazing to touch the stars
When you're so far down
It's amazing to feel so far
When you're in the center of town

Home is where the heart is
That's with you
I'm head over heals
That's what love can do
I love you

How to Save a Life

The large spruce lying lifeless in the park
Torn down by savage hands of selfish men
The sounds of night life as she crosses the dark
To escape from hell, to the church within

On her knees she prays, asks God in her heart
To help her from the violence that happens at night
She needs answers to keep from falling apart
She needs to know how to save her life

A spring rain falls as she carries her baby
On the old spruce stump ravaged by the unsatisfied
Now she prays on her knees with her child daily
And knows that God supplied the tears she cried

The only way to save a life
Is love and praise God and to do what is right

(I Don't) Change

Keep in mind, I'm like no one else
I will never change for another's satisfaction
I will keep my mind straight
It's between the Lord or you
To finish all that I started in my heart
Because it is all within Him or all you
And this sin I enclose in my thoughts
Can't be helped except to be released

I am Jeep

I am a lynx
I live in a cold world and I'm forced to adapt
I am a Jeep
I am strong and reliable
I am a hoodie
I am warm and comforting
I am Wednesday
I am stuck between the beginning and the end
I am a root beer float
I am a treat
I am the rain
I enhance life and I create disaster
I am a lily
I am not afraid of who I am
I am a balalaika
I come from a combination of different cultures
I am a trapezoid
I am rough around the edges
I am "Prayer of the Refugee" by Rise Against
I can have fun, but include a hidden meaning
I am fall
Solemn and depressing
I am Buffy
I fight against evil
I am mayonnaise
I am loved by some, hated by others
I am a lamp
I shine light on new ideas

I Care

Deep blue eyes piercing my soul
When I looked at them I felt whole
But you rejected possibility
You wanted someone else instead of me

The pain I feel is deep within
How tired I get, my fake grins
I wonder why you wanted to know me
And I tried to know you, but you had to leave

I don't know your feelings, I won't even try
But if it helps, I've wanted to die
I don't like to cry and I wonder why
This feeling won't end, it won't subside

Through these words and my steady breaths
I hope you know the truth so I can rest
I don't even care if you understand or not
Only that you care even if I don't understand

When you long to be yourself
I'll walk right beside you
And when you long to be loved and missed
I'll hold your hand tight and I'll miss you

I Cry

Secrets revealed after years of desperation
Piled on top of each other, quaint relations
Disgraces and traces of hidden worlds gone wrong
Like the lyrics of the oldies and new punk rock songs

I cry when I hear your voice after I hang up
I cry when I see your face, yet you've gone
I cry when I touch your face, nothing left
I cry when you feel me too
I cry cuz it's so wrong

Worlds unraveling truths, I'm retracting the leash
Together forever, I wish we could be
Frantically recalling all these missing memories
Left behind like a leper, only you could see

That I cry when I hear your voice, unsettling
I cry when I see your face, my poison to love
I cry when I touch your face, electricity shocks
I cry when you feel me too
Cuz your soul's up above
I cry

I Love Hate, I Hate Love

I'm writing this letter to you
I'm sending this letter to you
I'm waiting for a letter from you
I will never get a letter from you

I'm calling you
But it says, "You have the wrong number"
You must hate me
At least I tried

I'm sitting in this dark room
Developing pictures of you
I've got my darts ready
And now I've got my target

I'm sitting on this rooftop
But I'm not hiding like a sniper
I'm just waiting for the day to come
Til you leave my life so I can forget you
And I won't come down until then

I Know

Your words are followed by iconic bouts of sadness
Your memories seem to be the only thing that's timeless
And I know
It's not easy to be alone like you are
And I know
That it's so hard to deal when you're so far

You limit your message to simple words alone
You say what you need with a quiet tone
And I know
You can be what you so long
And I know
You cry when you don't seem to belong

Now you're dead and I have no one left
Now you have left and I feel like I'm dead
And I know
I will see you in days soon to come
And I know
Tonight we unite to where we came from
I know

I Love the Way

I love the way you smile
I love the way you talk
I love the way you make me feel when I don't think I should live at all

I love the way you comfort
I love the way you are
I love the way you look at me when I don't think I have a heart

I love the way you laugh
I love the way you hug
I love the way you make me fly out of this hole (of depression) I've dug

I Miss You

I cannot breathe, I cannot see
I want to hear, all you have to say
But when I find you, I forget
All the things I wanted to say
I hold your hand, I hold my breath
You close your eyes, I close my heart
You do your best, I give the test
I want you near, but I fail you
I want you, I need you
I miss you with all my heart
I had you, I lost you
I miss you more than life itself

I Need

I need my tummy filled
I need my mom and dad
I need water, water, water
I need not to be sad

Where is the food my tummy likes?
Where is my mommy and daddy?
Where on this dry dark place is there water?
Where is my smile I once had?

Why can't I eat when I'm so hungry?
Why can't I see my mommy and daddy?
Why does my spit not suffice my thirst?
Why do these people act so bad?

I need a light, O hope, my life back
I need to be loved and I need comfort
I need not the beatings, the seeings I see
I need not to hold a crust of bread for even dessert

I just need home, mommy, dad, food, water
I need not to be sad

I Notice

I notice
you seem stuck
in comatose
I can't reach you
in your reality
I hold on still
to your corpse
that fades away
holding your fingertips
that I know will only blow away
I feel the storm raging inside me
and I know that
you don't feel it
you're stuck
in your narcotic unconscious
you have become
your own glass house
throwing rocks
hard
at yourself
destroying yourself
and I notice
you seem stuck
in Lucifer's trap
your own demise
little by little
you know that these highs
are digging a hole
and every crash
is deeper
and will only get deeper
and when you finally
try to get out of that hole
you will find yourself

chained
to your drug
your addiction
and the only safe place
you will ever find
when you're all by yourself
is the hospital bed
where you are
drug deprived
and dead to the world
but when you open your eyes
and turn to see who
has stuck by you
since the day
she met you
you'll see me

Ice Alone

It feels like cold, freezing
Ice water as blood
Turning slowly
Becoming hard
Like life
Like fishing
In icy liquid
Going down
Deeper
D
   E
     E
       P
         E
           R
But finding nothing
Everything is there
Nothing is shown
Nothing is revealed
Faith thrown

I'll Stay Faithful

Even though you're not next to me and
You're away from me
You're inside of me
My eyes close and I cry
And you guide my choices
My footsteps

Even though you're so far away from me
I still hold your hand
And I'll keep holding it
I'll close my eyes, cry, and keep holding it

Even though I'm not perfect
You accept it as I accept you
Perfection is not achievable in our hands
But this way I feel is as close as I can get
So, I'll close my eyes, I'll cry, I'll hold you hand
And I'll accept our love
Our perfection

In Memory

Best friend, baby girl
I love you so much
You're my whole entire world
But when you left me
I felt so alone
Without you, I'm so dead
A grave is your new home
I'm left to live
All by myself
No one to talk to
To one to help
Best friend, baby girl
I love you so much
You're my whole entire world
You were my only crutch
And now I'm falling

In the End

When I told you that I loved you
I didn't mean what I said
I like you so much
But true love was dead

I can't tell you
How much your words hurt
But they did and now you've lost me
I can't tell you
How much your words hurt
But they did, they hurt deep

So I'm telling you straight up
We're through
I'm sorry it had to be this way
I bet you're sorry, too

Injustice

Was it not enough to take away my friends
You had to go ahead and continue
Well congratulations on a job well done
You keep on going, now my new best friend moved
And now I can't think of any bad memories
It's all that's good that remains, which is even worse
All that is considered passion is fading away
Making my mind into a contagious and depressing curse
And now my heart is confused and sick
Confusing and sickening my remembrance
I can't even see your face anymore
Only your eyes, the last time I saw your glance
I hate you more than ever as I love you
I miss you more than ever as I wish you were dead
The only way I'd weep with a cause
The only time I'd have to let go
You've chained me off this high building
And once it finally collapses, I will give up
I'll fall and I'll fall to a death of easiness
I'll fall to the ground, the ground and my body will be one

Kissing Misery

time disappearing sharply as my thoughts form into shapeless wonders
trying to wrap around endless ideas like love death God
my mind in bedlam, focusing on several nothings for hours
concentrating on everything and nothing, all the same
hypocrisy sways on porch swings in the middle of a hot august tornado
sanity dwindling like a hot sticky sundae, melting
changing constantly, yet confused by hardness of a plastic cup and lid
sticky, sweet, rotting inside me
like the feeling I get when I settle for nothing less than the best
what if my best isn't good at all
in fact, what if it's the worst
what if the beauty of love is contorted by the disgrace of sin and lust
what if happiness is being drowned by internal cues to hate yourself and
everybody else
what if I kissed misery on its lips and wrapped my arms around distrust
what if he wrapped his arms around me too
then what would I do
what could I do
what would happen if he, if he was you

Kissing With Eyes Wide Open

If

the eyes are the mirror to our souls
and
If looking into them makes you feel whole

If

eyes are the reflection of past regret
and
If

looking into them makes you forget

If

the eyes are the symbol of you and me
and
If

they are the only way you see
his soul that makes you whole
the regret that makes you forget
you and me, all I can see

Why don't we kiss with our eyes wide open?

Label You Cruel

It's quiet, but still footprints echo
Among corridors and empty classrooms
Secrets hiding behind pillars and corners
Trying to catch a glimpse of the past and today
Protecting myself from possible pain
From irreversible shame
Footsteps appear to sound closer
And closer
So close
Until finally it gets drowned
Because it's beginning to rain
And the sound of your voice
That's so far away
Is driving me crazy
Making me insane
It's the sound of your voice that I crave
The beat of your heart that I crave
The shock from the touch that makes your heart beat in pain
Cuz you know it's not true
You know what you do
You kill me inside
Cuz you know I am shy
And for that I label you cruel

Laced With Arsenic

I'm watching you slowly, but I follow you fast
I'll blow your freaking brains out with a single blast
I'll take your life away from you as you did mine
I'll haunt you and I'll taunt you
You'll lose your freaking mind
But don't worry about that, it's safe for now
But now covers now, not tomorrow night's frowns
I've been watching you lately, frown is my crown
My goal is to kill you, bring you down
I'm good to my word, I'll keep my vows
But you don't know a dang thing, I'm in your house
You take a sip of vodka, I whisper more
I sprinkle a little arsenic, sip, you're on the floor
Don't worry about a thing, darling, I'm still here
Don't worry about a thing, death is near
Unconscious and lonely, imprisonment homely
You're hopeless, you're still deathless . . . for now
But for now covers now, not tomorrow night's frowns
Funny thing is I'm you and I'm in your house
For now . . .

Last a Lifetime

Frankly, I think I've told you enough
You're wasting your time chasing me
I've told you a million times
You've got to play rough
You've got to get your hands dirty

Just a heads up, I am not a tease
But you will have to get on your hands and knees
Digging up past regret and ask God for forgiveness
Living life in righteousness

God is not an assignment that you put aside
Once you get on this roller coaster, you're on for the rest of your life

Left in Silence and Tranquility

He left a little bit ago
We talked for a long time
I lost track of the hours
And then I fell behind

He told me that he loved me
But we couldn't make it work
We tried so hard the months before
But all I got was hurt

My mind was rushing awkwardly
Spinning around violently
And now the silence aches
Inside I'm dying silently

He left a little bit ago
His message was clear
And now I stare in tranquility
At the image in the dirty mirror

He told me he loved me
But we couldn't make it work
And so I stare at my mind's wonders
As my heart breaks, oh it hurts

Legends of the Lost

Dear,
I'm afraid I have to go.
Everything I've ran from is catching up to me.
I do, so much, I love.
You.
But the time has come for me to depart.
And you can't come with me. I'm gone.

Everything I own now is yours, except my grandmother's old suitcase.
I've only brought a Bible, some pictures, and some letters and poems you
    wrote me.
But I don't need anything else, not money or clothing.
Only me and my memories.
You could find me if you tried, but if you love me you won't.
I just hope you understand that this is my choice.

Yours Always,
Love

P.S.
You'll be a father in nine months.
Please understand that I couldn't let you know a lot of things about
    my surreptitious life.
Our marriage can last forever, but I understand if you hate me.

P.S.S.
I do, so much, I love.
You.

Levels of Deceit

The thought that are running in my head
I bet you don't know a single one
Because you never pay attention
And you think I have all the fun
But look where you've gotten and look where I am
I've made it farther than you've ever been
I try to succeed and to do what is best
While all you even try to do isn't what you said
You play that game you always do
You say you'll be a bit better
But, after hours of working hard
You haven't done nothin' but make love letters
The lies that you told me were worse than ever
I wish I never met you, but then I wouldn't know
What it's like to be deceived

Life is Like an Open Window

Life is like an open window, you come and you go
You can't see the future, but you can see through
The world can break it or keep it untouched
You don't know the old things, but you learn new
It can rain above and pile snow below
It can keep you warm, but also cold
Opportunities rush by, but sometimes make it in
Someday that opportunity will let you in
You come and you go for the world doesn't care
If you come broken, the pieces you'll share
But if you're kept together, selfishness will arise
Life is like an open window, you got to close it sometimes

Life Label

The title
I was given at birth
is nothing
a name
no meaning
no symbols
only individually given
unique
the same
a hidden story
of abusers and abusee
a lifetime of pain
resulted in two
in the womb
a unit
together
and alone
Misty Rose and Amanda Michelle
versus
Saleena Elizabeth and Salisha Darlene
neither fit
better as
Mylie Marie
and
Eleanor (Ellie) Paige
beauty in two
meaning in unity
flames of life
ignited by the first thing
a name
the title
I was given at birth.

Life on the Lips of Lucifer

Tomorrow and tomorrow and tomorrow
Creeps in this petty pace from day to day
Always seeing through this light of time
Fretting the moment before an action changes the future
Changes the course of everyone's fragile lives
Until the one day everything ends
It will, one day, all end
Make a move, I dare you
You will die, I promise you
She died, she lost her life, a fall in this moment of time
When you light a path with your soul
You live for the sake of another's happiness
You supply their emotional helplessness when you die
And you will die, I promise you
Make a move, I dare you
Nothing can stop the blade of God from severing reality
Because God holds a knife at your throat
He is the light of your soul that lights the path
But a blow from his mouth will dissolve life, turn out the light
And a swift movement from left to right with a knife
Can and will end every single one's life
So life's illusion, meaningless, ends in God's swift slit

Limits

They say, "The sky's the limit."
But they add laws
They cage up the tigers
But they still have claws
You can't hide the truth
Not from anyone's eyes
They'll find out eventually
But they'll still say goodbye
Safety first, speeding paramedics
Runaway prisoners, speeding cops
Safety first, faster than limits allow
Safety first, snipers hiding on rooftops
They say, "The sky's the limit."
But they add laws
They cage up the tigers
But they still have claws

Living Words

If I could put my hand on your chest
And feel your heart beat
I could close my eyes and fall asleep

If the only thing you did for me
Was make me feel alive
I could finally hold my breath and expect to die

If I could hold in my tears
Until you were there to comfort me
I could never cry at all

If I could take back everything I've ever said to you
I'd do it now before you caused me pain
My downfall

Loss

My most recent emotion
Got me floored, cornered
Loss, lost
Tears are permanent scars
Weakness releases
My last goodbye seemed surreal
My last cries
Moments ago
Love is a passion
Concealed in a heart
Pure as birth
Lost at death
Missing you as days last
Cancer certain for death
Last of open eyes
Now in heaven, permanent rest
Kissed on the hand, kissed on the cheek
Smiled before she died
Missing is what she'll be
When she's put under

Lost Among the Dead

Turn around and look at yourself deep
Who are you, what will you be, not me
Because one day you're someone, the next you're not
The next you'll be the one we forgot
Nothing for sure, except inevitable death
The one thing I long for, eternal rest
But when will I feel better, when will this end
All this pain I feel, when did it begin
Nowhere I look seems to help it subside
This depression I feel, like an ocean's tide
But worse
Sometimes I see her, actually I do a lot
But she'll never come back, for sure she will not
She's like my guardian angel, at least now she is
Just a lost soul that forever I'll miss

Lost in Myself

I've given up on myself so many times before.
I can't remember why
It doesn't even matter anymore
I just want to die

There are things you can't understand
Like death and God and love
Down the hourglass falls sand
And I'm left staring at the ceiling above

I've lost myself inside myself
I can't begin to see
Why I feel like hell
Why I can't let myself be

There's nowhere left to hide
Where I did, I disappeared
Once I said goodbye
I lost myself in tears

I've failed at living
I can't do anything right
Maybe I'll succeed in dying
Good night

Love: A Sonnet

We face each other as you stand in the doorway
And we walk slowly away from each other, fingertips touch
And I love you with my life, I wish you to stay
But you have no choice, you have to go, I will miss you so much

Our hands are slipping, I'm holding on so tight
But we go on our separate ways, tears creep
And if I could look into your eyes, we would make it right
We could fly together in the sky at night or in a hole so deep

However we feel, however far away, I love you
Whether your breath on my cheek or your voice in my ear
Or a letter in my hand or nothing at all, I hope you love me too
And one day I hope we could be together, we could be near

No matter the length of the days, we will be apart
You may like that, but no matter what, you will always be in my heart

Love Isn't

Love isn't just something you go by
Love isn't something that makes me cry
Love isn't a thing that should make you lie
After you give me the butterflies

Love vs. Hate

Skin so soft
Eyes shut tight
Tuck me in
With a kiss goodnight

Hands are shaking
People meeting
Say hello with a
simple greeting

Skin so soft
Eyes shut tight
Your coffin lies
Within the light

Hands are shaking
People meeting
Say hello without
Conceiting

Love You Left Me

Love you left me
Now I'm here alone
You used to save me from myself
You made sure the light was shown
For me but
You killed yourself so many times
Before you actually did
So when you pulled the trigger
You were pretty much used to it
You never saw the light, only the darkness
You numbed yourself with many pills
You gave up on yourself
Love, you left me
Your dead body, my last memory
And the reason I'm not crying
Is because I've cried for you before so many times
And I wanted you to see I cared
But now that you're dead
I can't care
When you left me
Love, you left me dead

Lovesickness

A feeling I have only felt once
Forever afterward
A sadness of angst
You're gone
Love lasts forever
I want it to stop
Fade away
Like a rotting rose
Decaying slowly
To end like waking up
From a nightmare
Sweating from relief
It's over
No longer haunting
But the memory never fades
It's faint like a heartbeat
Slower, slowing, slowly, until it's over, it remains
Love is forever
So is the pain

Lured by Love

You told me all the things I wanted to hear
I thought my life was coming together
But in the end, I saw the truth
I knew you were dead forever

The lies you told me
The days that went by
The fire that exalted me
Until the day you died

The only thing that kept me sane
That kept me together in hard times
Was the love that you gave me
Was the sneaky tone of your rhymes

You told me all the things I wanted to hear
I thought my life was coming together
But in the end I saw the truth
I knew you were dead forever

Married Until the End

Long black dress, pale white face
Wedding bells chime, today's the day
Distant sounds, lifeless love
Tears on her face, just a slight shove
Till death do us part, she'll cry
Say, "I do, I do", but let's hope she won't tonight
Irrational, yet unconditional, she will say it, "I do"
But everyone gathered at the congregation knows it's not true
One kiss on the cheek, one placed on her lips
One kiss placed on her forehead, counting down anger's tick
Down goes the veil, down toward her eyes
Cover up the pain, the tears, her forced compromise

Long black dress, pale white face
Church bells chime, today's the day
Distant sounds, lifeless love
Tears on his face, it was just a shove
Death did its part, shoved in the dark, he cries
Broken-heart, no one to save her, she died
One tear on the cheek, one placed on her lips
One tear placed on her forehead, look what he did
Down goes the lid, down over her body
Cover up the pain, the tears, her remains
Into the ground, six feet in counting
Ended violently, ended at last
Till death do us part, till death at last

Middle of the Highway

In the middle of the highway
Is the calmest place of all
But you don't know that until you see
That the line has not been drawn
Until you feel the wind
Blowing across your face
You cannot tell
That the middle of the highway
Is the calmest place

Mirror Reflection

I look at you, but then I see me
When you speak, the words flow off my tongue
We are similar yet nothing alike
I wonder what's going on
The mirrors in from of me, beside me, behind me
Help me cover them up
I don't want to look at them
The vanity is just too much
The girls and guys are there
Looking through the mirrors
Don't look through the mirrors, I say
Look at their eyes or you'll pay
If you see beyond the mirrors
You'll see more than life alone
You'll see the mind, the love in their hearts
Instead of the fire and instead of the burning parts
For the reflection of the outside will never compare to the beauty inside

Misfits

Brown
A tree alone
An empty forest
A dead squirrel
Unpacked boxes cluttering the house
The hair that hides my eyes
The crap I deal with
Brown

Grey
The clouds of a dull midday
Worn concrete
Pencil marks of sad doodles
Used silver
The alarm clock screaming
A heart that's been broken
Grey

Black
Lost hope
My ever closing eyes
The nighttime reassurance of nothing
Drunk driving accident
Devil hiding
Death
Black

White
Innocence
Taking advantage of
Blank pages
My fading skin
Behind these walls
Slipping away
White

Misleading Love

You've spent the last dime on drugs
Haven't you heard of hugs, not drugs
You can lean on me if you need
But you don't have to do that to bleed
Why can't you see these are bad addictions
Your mind is set on the contradictions
Your blonde hair dyed black, your clothes torn apart
You're in the trap, the dark
There's old letters in ashes on the ground
The time you've spent with the wrong crowd
Your body is used by different designs
But I think you're simply divine
You can always change your ways
Before it's too late
I'll stand by your side, I'll be the one who made your try
Who deleted your desires to die
Who weakened your heart, made you cry
I held you tight on rough nights, when the big dogs would bite
Like tonight
The feelings you've felt, the thought filled
The ones deleted by those pills
But I'll throw them down the drain
I'll cry with you in the rain
I'll help you, I'll wash the pain away
And make you happy till the next days

Mixed Up and Nowhere to Go

I haven't thought about you in a while
You're the thoughts below my consciousness
Always there, but never realized
Until now
Because I can't stop thinking about you now
I can't stop fretting what will soon happen
I don't believe in myself anymore
Not since I fell in love with you

They all tell me it's nothing
These butterflies are normal
They come with infatuation
They will soon fade

But now that I know you are real
Now I know that I don't have to worry
I worry all the time, I can't do this
Everything is changing
Even the rage that I have buried deep
Is seeping through every emotion
Sneaking out like a poison released through my veins
And I'm left with the mess

Mosquitos

The thing I hate is mosquito bites
Too bad they're not afraid of heights
They bite you all over the place
Blood is the only thing they like to taste

The thing I hate is mosquito bites
Benadryl on my body is an awful sight
They heal very slowly when I say
"Hey you mosquitos, you're gonna pay!"

Most Precious of Time

the most beautiful of moments
life's entirety
the key of forgiveness, repentance
resilient time of faith, forgotten, one
night of chilling breeze, torturing pain, and
swelling heat

she lies on the rough, prickly hay, night's
arrival
novel adventures of a delicate neonate
finding his way to freedom and light
first cries, wiping vernix from his pink cheeks
swaddled closely to his mother's bosom

life lies hidden in the dark manger
but stars know, lead
many to follow, to fear
the king
gossamer hair on top of baby Jesus' head
merely awaiting surmise
secretly gifting a holy life

silence surrounds the helpless infant
but soon he'll be surrounded by
worships and cries of relief, released
as he's placed into the arms of me

Mother of Mine

Make each day a blessing, dear mother of mine
I love you with my heart, my soul, my mind
Fill your day with laughter, so laughter will fill your day
I hope we'll be happy, I hope and I pray
Our new beginnings, soon to start
To be a love of family that will be in our hearts
To charity, to church, to make happiness fill our hurt
So let's not remember all our tragic pasts
But bring memories to our future at last

My Annabelle

There are no words to describe this
No words at all can tell
How deeply this has wounded me
How deep I sunk in hell

And now I'm left with emptiness
My bedside empty, bare
Leaving me wishing
That your body was there

My love, I miss you deeply
More than words can say
I miss you more and more
Getting closer day to day

I long for you to stay safe
I long for you to be
My one and only forever
Until I'm home free

My Boy

Do you ever wonder why I love you
Trust me, it's not the looks
I love the way you treat me
In the short time it took

My Couplet

My sister fell in the water
The lifeguard fell in after her

My Dark Place

I hide in my dark place, it's dark and it's silent
It helps me calm down, to keep quiet
To cry by myself, to laugh in the open
To keep my life on down low, while I'm
Trying to cope and
To help me relieve my anger somewhat safely
And to bring my emotions back to safety
To daydream alone about things I can't stop
I go to school, but each day it's harder to adapt
I hide in my dark place, alone, no one else
Will be here
No one else home, no home
No friends to watch my tears pour
To remain alive, my heart's desire
And to talk and laugh with eyes in tears
To know home isn't anywhere near anymore
My life has changed, I know
I can't know, don't want to
To daydream alone about the things that bother me
Brings tears, pours down, like a storm
My body's storm, it's still going on
And on and on and on, no end in my
Dark place

My First

My first breath of life
I took one night
Began when wanting free

My sister lying right beside me
As I left
Toward the light

When I went to a box
That felt like a cage
Hard, clear, and empty

That box was life I had
To escape it
And start anew

My Froggy Sonnet

What do you think the little frog would say?
The one that lives down at the shiny pond.
Would you ask him if he had a nice day?
Or would you ask him if he's seen beyond?

What do you think he would say back to you?
Would it be a lot or nothing at all?
I think he would say, "I'd like to meet, too."
Do you think he thinks, "You're a bit too tall."

What he really said was, "Can you help me?"
I had asked him, "What do you want help with?"
He said he thought the pond was really filthy.
I told him he needed to solve a myth.

But don't ask what that myth would have been
Because I ran out of ink in my pen.

My Guardian Angel

Can you be my guardian angel
Can you take my pain away
Can you take away my tears
And can it be your lips that I taste

Can you be my guardian angel
Can you fight off all my fears
Can you hold me under moonlight
And promise we'll always be near

Can you be my guardian angel
Can you walk me far away
Can you move me from my sadness
And make me forget yesterday

Can you be my guardian angel
Can you listen to my fears
Can you tell me what you don't like
And I promise I'm all ears

Can you be my guardian angel
Can you tell me everything
Can you listen to what I tell you
And trust me with anything

My Guardian Angel 2

I'll be your guardian angel
I'll tell you everything
I'll listen to what you tell me
And I'll trust you with anything

I'll be your guardian angel
I'll listen to all your fears
I'll tell you what I don't like
And I'll be yours for countless years

I'll be your guardian angel
I'll walk you far away
I'll remove you from this sadness
And I'll melt your memories away

I'll be your guardian angel
I'll kill your fucking fears
I'll hold you under moonlight
And I'll always be near

I'll be your guardian angel
I'll take your pain away
I'll kiss away your tears
And you will be the only one who my lips will taste

I'll love you forever girl
Even after I'm dead
Cuz when I'm buried underground
You'll still be in my head

My Heart

You poured my heart in a blender
You've smashed it with a brick
You've diced it with a butcher knife
And you've used a needle, little prick

You've squeezed my heart with your fingers
Ran the blood in my hair
You've thrown it off an airplane
And watched it fall, how fair

You've carved your name in my eyelids
So I sleep and I see your name
And you slit my throat every time I kiss you
So my love feels like pain

You've whispered your name so loud
It's all I can hear
You've bitten my neck so hard
It's like I'm a vampire with tears

You poured it in a cup
And drank it like a shake
You grilled it over fire
And ate it like a steak

My Heroic Couplet

My favorite class is creative writing
My favorite teacher, I'm still deciding

My Journey

Plunged under darkness of water
Pulled out as a new creation
Father, Son, Holy Spirit
I thank God for my salvation

Once so tired, depressed and all
But I opened my eyes, quiet awakening
Now I see the world in its beauty
Yet the temptation's power is sickening

I'm walking along my journey with God
But sometimes I feel like giving up
So now I'm putting into words
My journey
So my beliefs will not be corrupt

I feel alone, I want to be a disciple
But every time I try to open my eyes
They close up to me, don't want to believe
And I just don't know why

I'm walking along my journey with God
But sometimes I feel like giving up
So now I'm putting into words
My journey
So my beliefs will not be corrupt

My Limerick

Last week, the new baby arrived
Yesterday the daddy died
The baby cried
The toddler whined
Today, we're all trying to stay alive

My List of Love

long walks on the beach
sand in your toes
drawing with your finger in the sand
love quotes
dancing in the rain
hiding painful tears
looking on your past
remember painful years
looking in your eyes to find the truth
this is what it's like in teenage youth
Romance, fantasize, pain, trust, faith.
Devotion.
Affection.

My Lunch

In the lunch line
Where it begins
Getting slowly closer
In the auditeria
With my lunch
Finding a seat
In the auditeria
Eating lunch
Noodles and potatoes
In the auditeria
Smelling my lunch
Warm roll and milk
In the auditeria
Talking to friends
Finishing my lunch
In the auditeria
Hearing the bell
Taking up tray
In the auditeria
Where it all ends
Getting slowly closer
In the hallway
Going to class
The class that I attend.

My Memories, My Grandma

Roses are red, the color of courage
To make it through
Violets are blue, the color of the tears I cry for you
Sugar is sweet like the love you have for everyone
And that's why we think you're the greatest

My Quatrain

I've traveled those valleys
I've hiked in those trails
I've swam in those waters
I've died in those hails

My Questions

I've tried so hard and I know my heart
But why do I have so many questions
I sit around and think of you and wonder
Why my soul thirsts for something better
I cry for you, I miss so much
The times I actually had you
But now, I ask so many questions, so
Have you ever loved me? Will you ever be?
The person I've always needed, a part of me?
Do you feel for me as I do you? The world is yours,
So will you share it? Would you kiss my cheek if
It'd make me feel better? Would you hold my hand for
No reason? Would you say you loved me?
Would you mean it?

My Rocky

Son, I know you're tiny
Son, I know you're small
But Daddy loves you so much
Sand, stars, and all

Son, I know you're growing
Son, I know you're great
But Daddy wants you to know
That I'm coming home someday

My So Long, Farewell

I want to say goodbye, you're dead and gone. These are the missing whispers that I no longer hear, here they are, here they die

Boys saying they love you, they don't even know what love is as long as they can slither their slimy hands in places you don't want them to

The girls you think have your back, but they betray you when you need them most, you don't even see it coming, then they attack

Change is another thing I wish to say goodbye to, you hate to move all over, you just want to stay in one place for once. You want to connect, to be understood, but you move again. I HATE change.

The things no one understands, you tell not a soul, scared you'll tear everything apart, like you were savagely torn apart

Death that sneaks behind you, snatches you from life's hands and drags you to heaven at the same time, I'm being dragged to hell and trying to hold you up, hold you alive

You slip and die

And I'm the one left to put together the pieces
I'm the one left to say goodbye

Negligence

I recall smelling burning leaves and
a barbeque
the heat of the sun and the flames
and smoke
I felt smothered, all I could do
was choke
but this bitter feeling was not at
all new
I soon tasted the blood in
my mouth
bitter from iron
and decay
feeling forgotten from
firing away
your fists are raw, but you
posture stout
your voice echoes throughout my
unstable mind
I can't seem to forget how all your words
ran together
but how the meaning could seemingly
last forever
I hate you! You're stupid! I love you! You'll always
be mine
I believed all your lies, I saw past the
violent screams
I came back each time and trusted
your persistence
each time you broke me down, I had
no resistance
and each night I pray I'll awake from
this dream

New Hobby

I just did it
What I said I'd never do
The lines on my wrist
All fresh and new

Blood red and silent salvation
New wounds on God's creation
It hurt a little, not too much
Just a simple razor, my skin touched

New pain marked by old memories
What I can't have, I punish myself for
Living in fear of what I'll lose
Never knowing what "friend" will shut the door

I cry for no reason
I dread each passing season
Who will continue to love me
Who will give up when they see

I cause myself pain
The only I control
Water over fire, blood for life
Not yet has my blood been shown

My secret pride shed
My recent lust removed
My lies untold
The friends I won't lose

My ready redemption, my rescue
My life, my loss
My deadly disease, desired deliverance
My death

But I did it, it's done
My wrists, wrongdoing, wrath
But I am not gone
I'm here and I suffer, not gone

So if you love me for me
For who I am
You'll accept this like the rest
Without sympathy, apologies, nothing

No Way Around It

It's bright and early in the morning
Under my gloomy head
I can't decide what I'm going to do
All I want is to go to bed

I know I will die sooner or later
I wish it would come now
Because either way I'm a loser
Either way, I'll figure out how

Cuz people tell me I'm awesome
But I can't find it in me
I don't see how that is who I am
I can't see that in my reality

There's no way around it
Trust me there's not a way out
There's just one way down this short road
And I'm dead just about

Not Really

It doesn't feel real at all, only a faint memory
I can barely see your soft, pale face
I can barely remember those last days
Crying alleviates the pain, numbs the longing
Letting go is hard, I'm not ready, don't force me

It doesn't feel right anymore to keep senseless memorabilia
I can barely get rid of your printed pictures
I can barely find a strong enough elixir
Letting go is hard, I'm not ready, don't force me

It doesn't feel fair anymore, a lifetime of losing
I can barely hear hope now, losing life
I can barely hold on before I fall, ticking time
Letting go is hard, I'm not ready, don't force me

It never felt good leaving all who loved me
I can barely remember a conversation
I can barely think silent contemplation
I can't say I didn't try, because I know I did
But letting go is hard, it's not really me
And letting go isn't easy, not really
Don't force me

Not Sure

I love your hugs
Since I don't see you much
And I think I like you
But I'm not so sure

I miss your touch
Since I feel a rush
And I think I like you
But I'm not so sure

I want to see your eyes
But in a way, it's your disguise
And I'm scared to like you
But you just push away, me away

I want to hold your hand
But in a way, you slip through, like sand
And I'm scared to like you
But you just push me, me away

One Day

If one day you let me draw your face
In the dark midnight sand
I would kiss you on your lips
And push you away

If one day you let me write your name
On the deep ocean waters
I wouldn't stop until you stayed
I would drown before I let go

If one day you let me cry for you
Admist a brightly lit fire
I would slowly put the flame out
Tears by flame, one by one

If one day you let me love you
Anywhere in the world
I would do it
Right now

One For All and All For Nothing

The battle rages on
It's just me and myself
I can't help but to cry
My life's a living hell

But I walk ahead
My head held high
Someone may need me
To save their life

In the subtlest of ways
I surrender my love
Just to make sure others
Make it through the times that are tough

Because without me alive
With many others dead
One person may not be saved
They may die in red

The battle rages on
It's one for all
All for nothing
Living for a person to save another
Living for one is living together

One Too Many Times

One too many times
I've been let down
I let my heart get stomped on
One too many times
I let myself love you

One too many times I forgot
How that feeling made me feel
But now as the love I once knew so well
Lets me down
My hard heart hardly know what to do

One too many times I ran
From the only truth that I know
I wish everyone I knew would just understand
My feelings are cold
My feelings are lost as I begin again

One too many times I let go
Of all the things that made me this way
This is the only strength I know
This is the only pain I control
This is the cleansing I need to be freed from the untold

One too many times I wasn't protected
From all the doubt, the hate, the fear
From all the wanting, the longing for you to be near
One too many times I fell from this world
And forgot how to get up
How to get rid of this fear

One too many times I told the truth
Everything I told you was true
Everything I said, every world I told you
But I shouldn't have made this move
Cuz now I can't free myself from
All the agony, the tears, so cruel

But too many times I gave up
I let the pain be enough
All I did was let nature run its course
And now my remains remains a corpse
One too many times
I wanted this to be my last night
But tonight is my last goodbye

Only Thing That Counts

One gift worth giving in a limerick
Thus explained
Is something many families lack, make them go insane
Something to let love roam
Somewhere to call home
One thing that God lets happen to help when you're in pain

Oppression Freed

The way your eyes reflect me
In a twinkle of anticipation

Your hands wipe my tears
Under a deep depression

Circumstances reveal our fate
Relationship guarded by life's oppressions

Your lips upon mine, hands together
Me on my tippy toes for you
While we're freed from past aggression

Overflow

Opening up to You day by day
And I apologize for so many things
I'm crying for the moment
But it is only for Him
Because I thrive to hear the Word
I want to drown in it

Kind of like my baptism
The power of the Father, the Son, the Holy Spirit
Emerged for a second, changed for eternity
Started emptily on this fulfilling journey

I thrive to see my growth
Planting seeds in hopeful souls
Changing and growing
Planting and sowing
Down this Christian River, I'll be rowing
At times, I'll be floating
But the whole time, I'll be soaking

Panic Attack #1

I don't know what to say right now
I can barely even write
Your face was in my mind all day
And I can't stand the sight

My cowardice is all I know
I don't know what you want
I'm trying trying trying hard
But poof now you're gone

I hate I hate I hate the way I seem
So out of control
I accomplished writing a note to you
That was my first goal

You have no idea how much I tried
To get each word perfect
But obviously it wasn't enough
And apparently my sociable wasn't worth it

Now I'm doubting and reconsidering giving up on everyone
One guy is never worth a damn
And giving up doesn't mean you've won

I've always been so hidden in the world
The world without you
But now that you know
I don't know what to do

I prefer to be underground
In the sense that you can't see me
Cuz now you know my heart sinks when I see you
And everyone thinks I'm crazy

Please Forgive Me

I have eaten
The chocolates
That went on the cabinet

The one
You were probably
Melting
For milkshakes

Forgive me
They were yummy
So mouth watering
And so rich!

Praise Poem (Death)

Under somber realities
It is a necessity of life, death
It is an overwhelming peace
It is an ending to a divine pain
O heavenly death, O definite demise
Time's way of cherishing a moment
Thank you for a piece of mind
A thought to be careful
O dark one
Creeping silently among young and old
Sick and well, all in the end
A sore time, grieving sweeps over
Sadness is a cloud, hanging dimly
O death like a darkness or a light
A permanent end
An accident
Natural way to let go
A truth of a beginning of an end
Where you lead us toward your light
As a sign of relief, home, heaven, or
As a hope of end, for a forever beginning
Nightmare, nourished by the hands of one, death
Burning fire, frozen ice, nothing beyond this point
O death, O promiser, O truthful one, beauty
Like rotting roses, like blood on the thorns,
And ending

Process of Plucking Petals

I feel as if every time I see you
I lose my thoughts and memory
I forget everything
It's just you and me

I go into shock when I see your face
It just isn't fair what you do to me
Teasing me with dreams of you every night
It just isn't fair how I can't control things right

As I gaze upon you as I simply walk by
It's like I'm holding a rose
Each time I see you, each day that goes by
I'm plucking the petals till the rose is just a stem
The simplest of beauty is shed
Taken away until the ugliness is displayed
Stripped down till the thorns resemble rage

But I ignore all the signs that scare me so
I just repeat the process of plucking petals off the rose
But I don't drop the petals because I can't let go
I can't step over them, I just give up hope

There can never be a you and me
Even though when I see you my heart skips a beat
And I can never hold your hand and call you my man
Because one time my heart will skip a beat
And forget to beat again

Puzzled

Your name makes me cry
And I am not afraid of anything
Invincible except by the look in your eye

As if you were a puzzle laid out
I'm still putting you together
Figuring out what you're all about

Sometimes I feel we're the only two
Put together first in a puzzle of life
But yet the other pieces lay astrew

Random

I like what I've done, even though I seem like my love's all gone
I take what I want and leave the rest behind
And wonder if they got what they wanted to find

Reality Check

Even though I'm crying right now
And my heart threatened what it desires
And even though I'm in love with you
The soul and mind I have are in the painful fire
Even though I sleep with monsters surrounding
Even though I wake with continuing nightmares
I remain in love with you
Even though my tears fall red
And my heart beats slow
I deny this way I'm headed down this winding road
And even though I smile at times
And my laugh threatens to break
And even though my being is in love with you
The soul and mind I have isn't fake
Even though I sleep with frozen wishes
Even though I wake with melting reality
I remain in love with you
Even though my tears fall wrong
And my heart beats at least
I deny how I've fallen down and remained there
I still love you, my light in dark
My love will never die, the only part in me alive

Reconsiderations

There're so many reconsiderations
You're just one of them
And I'm sorry I'm making this difficult
But I'm just so scared and confused

Going against myself, my family
Just for what never usually works
Each time I go for my heart, it gets broken
You will or you won't, it'll never work

Remember

Remember all the times
Think about how bad they hurt
Is what you said what you meant
Is what you thought the truth

Remember all the times
Think about how much you lied
Is what you said what you meant
Is what you thought the truth

Remember all the days
Think about what you want to say
Is what you said what you meant
Is what you thought the truth

Remember all the words
They hurt
Remember all the times
The lies
Remember all the days
What to say
The truth, the meaning, your words
They hurt
So think

Rocks and Needles

I'm afraid so
My teeth crack more each meal
And I swallow black coffee and bread only crust
I spread it with butter that tastes more like rust
I'm afraid so

I'm afraid so
Prick a pin into my skin
For health and good color
Stick a needle in my eye
To experiment with eye color
I'm afraid so

I'm afraid so
Narcissistic fade away
Color lost from day to day
Looking nice to take a right
Choosing life or you're gonna die
I'm afraid so

Sacred Philosophy

They told me time was the only thing that would ease my pain,
To rewind it like it never happened. But I feel it holding me,
Controlling my life like pain does.

They told me not to worry. Nothing would change that would kill me,
But I changed . . . and I left hope behind, leaving silent
Nightmares and funereal thoughts to baby-sit my ever-morbid mind.

They told me no one could hurt me anymore and that everything
Would be okay soon. But you hurt me each day I think. You won't
Grasp my pain, only my heart, my ever-broken heart.

They said I would get used to everything. I would just have to let go.
I can't forget my life. My home. My family of friends. I
Definitely haven't gotten used to not being around you. I haven't gotten
Used to you not being here with me.

I hope I never become "them", filling others with false hope.
Letting go is hard. I'm not ready. I need my own reality.
My world of truth.
But I need it to be with you.

Safety Box

Down the road, there was this place
It housed all my best friends
Who lived in houses that were placed
Under the dirt
They listened to my whispers through the rain
My enemies couldn't touch me here
They ran scared at the thought
My best friends held me in solace
Comforting me in this hell
They understood, my best friends did
But they excavated my bones one day
Sifted through my nonexistent soul
Until I turned to dust
Down the road, there was this place
I considered it my home
My house of silk and stone
I cried out every night, my voice
Carried through the wind
My enemies can't touch me here
They run scared at the thought
My family of rotting flesh and bones
Comfort me in this hell
They understood, they did
But they excavated my bones
Sifted through my nonexistent soul
Until I turned to dust

Said I'm Sad

My days have faded
In time they have gone
And now my life is shaded
My feelings are distraught
Bats fly at night
Doves in the morning
I don't know who I'm adoring
I'm so confused at this moment
I can't decide my love or hate
I don't know if this happiness is torment
Or if this is the right way to behave
It's not that I'm stupid
It's not that my love ain't from Cupid
And my day starts round dawn
I hold myself tight
Cuz if I let go, I might fall
I hold in my goodbye
Cuz if I say it, I'll start building my wall

Savage Lake

I asked you, "Would you save me
If I jumped in?" You said, "Of course."
I jumped in and you saved me
You were mad, I loved you more

But behind my back, I didn't know
That he never loved me at all
When the water ran over my head
I succumbed to death as I beheld the fall

The water salty and wet and dangerous
My heart flying out at each beat
I couldn't help but to notice his ignorance
Couldn't help to see that he didn't see me

The air aroused by nature, curiously rosy
Aromas of lavender and dirt desired
The trees waved southward, northward, there
But as his arm grabbed my belly, I felt fire

He dragged me from the water, raging and pissed
But I couldn't drown the thoughts to kiss
His arms so strong to save me from fate
But the only thing I didn't see was hate

I asked you, "Would you save me
If I jumped in?" You said, "Of course."
I jumped in and you saved me
You were mad, but I still loved you more

Scarlet River

Water running, smiles gone
I cut my wrists, now my life is done
Too much pain, too much stress
Now, my baby, you'll swim alone
I told you I'd die without you
You thought I was kidding when I said it was true
Bright eyes meet glum outcome
All that's heard is, "What have you done?"
Evidence on the floor of wrongdoing
Down the road left my dreams, unpursuing
Too protected, too untrusted
Too many lives left in disgust
Water overflowing, frowns begun
I cut my wrists, now my life is done
Too much pain, too much stress
Too many times my heart left dead
I told you I'd die without you
I proved my love to you was true
I've accomplished my life dream
Now I hope you follow through

School Wars

Is school a place of war?
Do you get scared when someone's at the door?
Little boys and army men,
Is war a game you have to win?
Footsteps pound the floor
Will you listen to seargents . . . . 1 . . . , 2 . . . , 3 . . . , 4 . . . ?

Seeing Isn't Believing

If seeing were believing
Nothing would work
We can't see God
We can't see love
We can't see order
I can't see you

If seeing were believing
Nothing would work
We can't see spirits
We can't see time
We can't see passion
But I believe in you

If seeing were believing
Nothing would work
We only see what we want to believe
So I continue to believe in you

I continue to believe in God
I continue to believe in love
I continue to suffice the order inside
So soon I'll be in heaven above

I continue to believe in spirits
I continue to believe in time
I continue to feel the passion inside
And I pray that soon you'll be mine

If seeing were believing
Nothing would work
We only see what we want to believe
So till the end of time
I'll always believe in you

Seeketh of You

I'm shaking and I don't know why
The liquid tears run down my cheek
I lay in bed, try not to cry
No one to comfort or understand me
The crayons fill the floor
The paper filled with crayon marks
I'll fall, I know, before I get to the door
I know for sure, all I see is dark
I know for you, how you feel
The way you comfort, your lips sealed
You won't tell a soul of what I've done
I know it's a mistake, but I can't run
They'll find me before it's too late
I'll be saved from my fearful fate
The one who died for ours
Gave the example of my final hours
I hope I'll get away, make my choice
I know I'll move away, speak my voice
You'll live for me and help me through
You'll seek some days, the days of new
I can't figure out why roses are red
Or violets blue or sugar sweet, but I know
That they are and it's because of you

Sleep No More

He's drunk right now
Screaming past his capacity
Pushing, punching, yelling
I'm tired and sad tonight
Yawning, breathing, crying
Trying to think, to sleep
Block the noises I hear
Trying to count one sheep
Block the noises, I hear so clear
Screams again, drinking
Too much anger I feel releasing
Runaway, runaway, flew, goodbye

Slow Fade

walking up steep hills with
spirits of loved ones
dead
writing about fantasy or
a reality gone wrong
life
reading about God and
how he loves us
religion
thinking about the impossible
straying away from family
moving
believing that love fades
and people go away
escape
finding love in mind
and in advanced math
school
driving no car now
but dreaming of Jeeps
liberty
sleeping next to demons
and an old baby doll
Xavier
hiding from the truth away
in this solemn coma
simplicity
revealing my complex mind
to the outside world
future
who will I be
I'll be me.

So Much Negativity

I'm the emptiness beneath the rainbows
I'm the blackness of the sea
I'm the one in the middle of the room
That you refuse to see

I'm the plague that destroyed the city
I'm the rage that grows inside
I'm the reason things are so bad
The reason you want to hide

I'm the darkness behind the moon
I'm the pain that stays aware
I'm the nightmares that consume you
The ones that never disappear

I'm the decaying of a body
I'm the sense that you're not here
I'm the disappearance of what's fair
And I am the reason that you fear

Sometimes

Sometimes, inspiration doesn't come from the heart
Sometimes, it perspires from the darkness apart
From all the things that happen in life
Apart from all the backstabbers and liars alike
Sometimes, generations of now starve
Sometimes the youth of tomorrow carve
Away all the sadness and gloom from their souls
Away all the gloom and messages take toll
Sometimes, the smiles we show do hide
The pain that we feel like a rollercoaster ride
Sometimes

Speed

One second
I feel like I'm under
A cloud of work and depression
Everything is running so fast and know
I
can't
reach
it all.
But yet I keep running
And getting more and more
Out of breath
Out of will and motivation
Out of reason
I can't get out.

The next second
I look up from my busy computer screen
and see
him.

A. Dream

Falling. Drifting. Alone. Now.
Everything. Is. So. Perfect.
I. Think.

I. Go. To. Where. He. Went.
Say. Hi.
He. Says. Don't. Be. Shy.
But. I'm. Not.
I'm. Scared. And. So. Happy. Heaven.

I. Thought. It'd. Take. Just. One. Time. To.
See. Him.
To. Know. I. Don't. Like. Him. Anymore.
But. That. Theory. Was. A. Joke.

As I got my. Thoughts back slowly.
I realized how. Surreal this was.
I hadn't see him. In over a year and a half.
And now.
Now.

He is aware that I like him a lot.
He knows but isn't afraid.
Accepts.

We talk about nothing and everything.
Mainly nothing.
His car. My dreams. His plans. My crush. On him.

Oh, what would I do. Just to hand out with him. To have him see I care
a lot. To have him care.

I would love to run into him. To see him happy. To know he's okay. To
know he always will be. To know that the pieces to my heart's puzzle isn't
missing anymore.

It's missing. I don't know what to do anymore. He's missing. There's
nothing I can do anymore.

A moment. Just one. That means everything. Is a moment you live for.
This is that moment. The one I continue to live for.

Stalked and Murdered

Follow me and stalk me down
Aim and fire, on the first round
Keep me bleeding, tears run cold
You don't want to do what you're told

Take it to the next level

You take out your handcuffs
Chains made of cannonballs
Hearts cuffed together, yet so alone
Twist and contort, my mind is sure to fall

You're still pushing to the limits

Your handgun like a paintball gun
Shoot, red, yet you're not dead
Not yet

You don't know when to stop

As I get colder, my tears won't turn off
As my body turns pale, barely I cough
This is the feeling I get because you're not here
And the key to the cuffs would be that you're near

States of Conciousness

Within the folds of sticky membrane
And skull
Lies the magic
Jibble-jabbled by creation
Of individuality and conformity
Of craziness or normality
To distinguish yourself from others
A mental puzzle
Not meant to be solved
Confusing even the wisest with a
Simple, complicating part of intelligence
Views on wit and perception
Differs on one cell to another
Controls and limits like calculus
In every mind
Yet differs like the imbecile and insane
A feeble-minded freak foretelling the future
The asinine wise guy who know all but tells
None
The intricate design
Surged beneath waves of electrical currents
Flowing steadily past the spine to limbs
Dreams or trances or meditation
In a stupor or a coma
Lethargic and hyperalert and frenzied states
Lost or out of control or wandering
Through the folds of curiosity of
The brain

Still

I'm in this state of calm
While you're lying in your coffin
The blood of your life on my hands
And now my heart is softened

I can't remember how I felt
Before your heart stopped beating
All I know is pain and numb
And now I can't stop bleeding

It's like I took your place in time
So many out to help me
But I just ignored the signs
Until I yelled, "God, save me!"

They dug your grave so very deep
To try to give you peace
But you ended up lower than before
Now you're my beloved deceased

Straight Jacket Feeling

Shadowy figures glare at me from the corners of my unexpecting mind
They poke and jab their probing fingers into my brain
Still they can't figure me out
They're flabbergasted

And I know that I cannot fathom heaven or hell
I can't feel life before this moment or after this moment
I want to remember that split second
The next

But they find me different
That's all I ever wanted to be
But now they just poke
They point and distort my image as a reflection behind this slab of glass

This hole of padded walls and straightjacket pajamas
House my nothingness, infinitely, lost in eternity
There isn't any other place to be
Except in this dream, my reality

I'm mocked by myself, alone I mock myself
My soul is painted on these white walls
My heart is beating to the tick of the tock
I'm a virgin who failed to read the signs

They're flabbergasted, that they are
And I won't remember one moment from the next
They point and distort my image as a reflection behind the slab of glass
There isn't any other place to be except in this dream, my reality

Stream

Water wading beautifully
Down a sun lit path
Trickling past the underbrush
Until it falls at last

And when it hits the bottom
Of the waterfall of life
It fades and mixes with the rest
Of bubbles, toils, strife

Stuck

I am stuck between now and then
I don't even care about later
And when you talk to me, pull me away
I feel like a pawn, a useless player
And when you ask me questions
I don't know how to answer
I'm too lost, alone, broken

I am stuck between you and hard times
I'm forgetting about you, my good times
And when you go to touch me
I shrink back to myself, untold lies
And when you shine your light on me
I hide, I cry, I hate the light, I die
I'm too lost, alone, broken

I can't break away, I try so bad
I take what I can, leaving so much
And when you end up fading away
I'll go back to begging for your crutch
To hold me up, like you've done
Giving me the balance I need, it's just enough
I need to be fixed, found by you

Stupid

I was stupid to fall into your trap
Why did you help me at all
If you never felt for me
Why did you save me

I was stupid to think like this
Cuz now that's all that's left
I wait for your arrival
Cuz you're all I'm waiting for

I was stupid to believe you liked me
If no one likes me here, why will they there
They are my everything, taken away until nothing
Missing pieces in this game of nothing

I was stupid to think I could fall asleep
Sleep was my only escape and now it won't come
Nightmares nor nothing, good gone gruesome
Tears fall from my empty eyes

I was stupid to think you'd come through
Anyone waiting for me will wait forever
Maybe forever wouldn't be enough
Just like my feelings, forever won't heal this pain

I was stupid to end my life this way
Cut off from existence entirely
Waited and waited, wanted and longed
Finally in the end, maybe I'll belong

Suicide Poem

He made sure to cover all the bases
Before he killed himself
He got all his pictures of her
Off every single shelf

Then he poured his bathwater
And made sure it was nice and hot
And he scattered all the pictures
On the fluffy floor mat

His parents had just went out of town
On their "Christmas vacation honeymoon"
And as soon as they left
He got the gun from their room

He lit all the candles that he could find
And put them on the bathtub sides
On the floor, the sink, the toilet seat
And he went to the kitchen to find a sharp knife

As he stood in the doorway staring at his fate
He began to cry, he knew this times was official
He set his note in front of the door
His parents had to know his decision was crucial

He closes himself in this dark death chamber
He places his feet into the water
He sits himself comfortably down
And for an instant he saw her

But as soon as he touched her face
It disappeared into folds of soft waves
He knew he had to do this
Today is his last day

He puts the knife into his palm
The metal is nice and warm, he kissed the blade of which he's about to be killed
He puts it slowly to his wrist
His dream is about to be fulfilled

He cuts down slowly, he feels no pain
He took so many narcotic pain relievers before his parents left
He barely know the blade is doing its job
He knows that his promise to God is going to be kept

As he finishes both veins, severing them completely
He grabs the heavy handgun, he feels he's getting weak
But he knows he has to shoot this gun to kill someone
To finish this job sweet

He pulls the trigger, but it does nothing
He feels he is so tired, so he fights the fatigue
He unlocks the gun and holds it to his head
And in one blast toward the wall, he is accomplished under bloody water and little mess

When his parents find his letter
They read it slowly
And when they open the door
They find their son dead among pictures of his girlfriend and in the middle
Her obituary

Suicide Vacation

The wind faintly whispers against my cold cheeks
The past threatening me
I break
I'm haunted by the ghosts of yesterday
I'm going to fly awake today, fly away
Go on vacation with suicide
She'll welcome me tonight
Together we'll fly, tonight in the sky

The wind is bitter, your nose is numb
The rain is calling, down from heaven it comes
Hiding the tears
You're haunted by thoughts of legendary fears
Like me, yet you don't know that I'm near, I'm here
Go on your way, you'll find me soon
Maybe you'll go on vacation with me too
Together we'll fly, both under the moon

The wind is silent, my breath is weak
Our pasts are frozen, our hands did meet
You hold me close
We're haunted by midnight monsters and mayhem most
I'm close to home, my solemn comatose
Go on, move on, get a hold of yourself
You tell me over and over that I could have gone to hell
Together we could, even now in your arms I melt

You don't know how much the wind whispers your name to me
You don't know how it drives me insane
You don't know how I love it to feel you so close
You don't know how much your heart is home

The Dating Proposal

You're all I can think of
For better or for worse
Is this a bad thing
Or can we make this work

I barely even know you
But it's you that I chose
To crush on for the moment
For our hearts to get close

But I'm scared of possibilities
Some are not that great
But I close out all negativity
And hope you say yes today

The Final Frontier

His eyes were the color of a stormy sky
His mind was like that of a tornado
His brain was like the aftermath of disaster
But his body remains calm, like the eye of the storm

The people couldn't fathom what it's like
They can't possibly know
All the things he thought in a day
Made him want to hide some more

And sooner or later, he'll hide
And he won't know how to escape
To come out of this freshly dug grave
That he came to fall inside

The Letter

Would you know me if you saw me
Would I recognize you
So many things are different
Except for me and you

I refuse to be the one everybody wants
Because that position has a price tag
If I conform to their standards
I'll be no better than those hags

I'm better than them in the fact that I'm me
I don't see anyone better to be
I'm better at hiding myself in the world
But I like how you can see

If you walked down a busy sidewalk
And I was walking down a narrow hallway
Both of us surrounded by the world
Would you ask if I'm ok, would you be ok?

Would we sit and talk for hours
If we met again one day
Or would we sit in silence
Enjoying each other's company

Would you reveal the pain in your heart
Would I tell you about my dark secrets
Would you accept me for me
Would you show me your scars

Would you know me if you saw me
Would I recognize you
Everything has changed already
Ever since you moved

I told you you'd be my friend way in the past
And I'm not willing to lie
We're both ready to break behind the glass
But I refuse to say goodbye

You mean the most to me than anybody else
And I hope you can see that's the truth
Ever since you left, I've been a mess
And I want you to know, I miss you

I dream and I think and I try to remember
All the things you've told me, in words, or in silence
I think about their meaning, I think about you
I want to go back to the past, rewind where my time was spent

The Naïve, The Wise, The Forgotten

The Naive
He's small and scared and alone
A fragile soul in this torturing world

He stands brave and powerless under the starless night
Away from his mother's grave, his father's fist
Away from everything that plagued his mind

He wishes upon the comet to help him through
He didn't know God was coming
He didn't know what to do

The Wise
He's small and scared and alone
A fragile soul in this torturing world

He stands brave and powerless under the starless night
Away from his wife's grave and his drunkenness
Away from his age, his wrinkling, his wearing sight

He is no longer wishing to the comet, he's praying to God
To tell him he misses his wife
To thank him for the cancer that will take his life

The Forgotten
He's small but he stands next to God
He's a fragile soul in this boundless heaven

He no longer stands at the edge dreaming of this fantasy
He lives it, breathes it, keeps it at heart
This eternity is a reality

He is no longer seeing that nothing changes because life and
death is a drastic step

The Naked Truth

I'm sorry you haven't heard all the rules
You ain't given freedom or none of the tools
You're more racist, you're less tolerant
At home, Upward Bound, that's where our time's spent
You judge from the outside, you threat from within
You think from every argument we expect to win
I scream back to get my point across
To make you listen cuz you think you're boss
But, to be honest, you get too drunk, you don't understand
You take all we have because you know you can
So, I'm here to tell you, life's filled with too many people like you
And I hope you change, I really do
I pray to be better, to do what is true
But, just cuz there's girls getting pregnant, getting drunk, doing drugs,
judging looks
I'm not one of them, I got morals, I got thoughts
I've got a mind and I plan to use it and improve during time
But let me live, let me learn, let me find out
What it's like to be my turn

The Only Path

The days last flood, I bid farewell
The stories I told, I no more tell
The tricks those boys play won't sell
The faults those girls fall to yell
No one understands nothing about
The times we go through, bring doubt
The water no more, it's nothing, all drought
They both scream and yell, all to shout
With the water's drowned, me underneath
I'm sorry to say, but I couldn't reach
The faith I had dissolved, now I teach
The love I had felt, disappeared when you preached
I tried to believe, to see what was right
To search for God and His hidden light
I found too late what I had done
But I want you to know I haven't won
I live through and through, night by day
The voice I use to speak is only mine to say
The floor with the water, limply lay
The light shown by God, lights my way

The Party

The party gets louder as I get quieter
And slip away
The party is distant, outside, away
I pray to escape
The party is getting darker, the moon is there
And so is my heart because nobody cares
I feel so alone because I try to reach out
But you close up your heart to me
So much I care, so much I want you to believe
But you curse the name that is a part of me
The party is bigger, like my heart just was
But I want to teach you His word just because
There is only one way to eternal life
In heaven, home, paradise
And it is through Him
I pray to escape, to get away
I pray to open your eyes
To what really matters
The party is getting slow
Talking goodbyes, white light, in paradise
I pray you'll believe before one day you die
So you, too, will live in such paradise

The Plath Effect

The day you died, I went into the dirt
Where I had no one around me, here
I can hide under this extra large shirt
As I cry, I suffocate in my tears
They drown me and kill me and flirt
With my fading heart, oh love that's not near

I used to know who you actually were, I'd flirt
With your soul, I could care less if your body was near
Because I saw through your words of dirt
And I'd call you each day to wish you were here
I missed you so much, even the smell of your shirt
And when you answered the phone, you could sense the tears

But one day, I called to remind you I had your shirt
The one with the wine stains and my bitter tears
You came over and found me, catatonic in the dirt
Of lost whispers, cold love, death so near
As you placed your lips on mine, removing broken glass from my hand
that flirts
With crimson beads of life on my wrists here

You saved me in my weakness, as I was tainted by innocent dirt
As I was dying, choking, asphyxiating, by my own tears
You weren't afraid to love me still, weren't afraid to flirt
With my weaknesses, your weaknesses, even with blood right here
You saw past me as I reproved myself over and over in your shirt
You saved me only because you were near

Slowly the days fade into nothing, death flirts
With time that's appealing to disappear, no longer near
I realize nothing anymore, I sit here cadaverous and inconsequential,
your shirt
On my weak, numb body, I'm falling with my tears
Fast and vulnerable, suddenly under the dirt
Until you pick me up, you're stalwart, you're here

I'm not alone anymore, I smell you, comforting, your shirt
It's cold and wet but my only safety from the devil that's near
Knowing that when you're with me, I can't flirt
With temptation, I can't lose this war with myself, you're here
On this dark couch in a dark room, away from dark dirt
You're here, and in the dark with me is where I love you, you love me,
you can't see my tears

The day you died here I went into the dirt
Buried near a glass, my blood, my tears
I died for you, missing your shirt, so with death did I flirt

The Thing I Never Told You

You were amazing, nothing could compare
Until I lost you
You were the apple of my eye, my chosen one
Until you left
You were my heartbeat, my pulse, my life
And now you're gone
Leaving me with the three words I never got to say
So now I'm silently craving to see your face again
So you know for sure
That I do love you

But you're gone

Thennow

a brown puppy lost in heaps of garage sale rubble
became my guardian angel when innocence left my existence at night
morning moon fading into a large hot jawbreaker in the unclear sky
family wrapped around a technologically advanced box watching Buffy
playing with backyard dirt and beautiful dog
and words
of music, of books, of poems, spoken reoccurrences tearing through
walls of
a glass house of sorts
soon forgotten in a mix of sound and fury
and silence
secrets hiding behind happy pictures
love becomes sin
our lives, a prison
he's now in prison

papers filling folders and the floor
buildings towering above me, I have to enter
clickclacking echoes through the narrow walls of hospitals, colleges, offices
professional act
soothing silence of loud music on MP3 in library
views from the trees are misshapen but beautiful, hopeless yet intriguing
permanent memories disappearing
and me in the middle of both said trees and buildings
torn between nature and reality and who am I really
the true answers gone missing and ancient
I have to find the new meanings, new answers while questions remain always
Now I face others' realities and yet I still don't care what they think
I'm me and I won't change for anyone

Thought Wrong

I thought it'd take one time
To see you
To show me I don't care
I thought wrong
I still like you
If not love
Teenage hormones uncontrolled

And to see you after
A year and a half
In all honesty
Nothing has changed
I'm still who I was but older
You're still who you've always been
But growing

So many words to say
In so little time
I space out, I can't think
For words to come out
I will not be able to forget you
I know it
You mean so much, I can't let go

To Thy One, Thy Only

What shall I say hence we meet again someday
How can I tell you how lovely you are
For thou has silent, but strong, mysterious eyes
Thou hast made my smile complete, my laugh loud

How
Do thou miss me, at all, if any
Have you found an equal to you as you are in my eyes
Has your heart beeneth broken as mine has

Can change taketh away something so strong
If thy feeling isn't mutual, can it stay
Doeseth time upon thy clock erase memories or happiness
Or pain
Or love

Tonight

I fell in this hole today
I didn't see it coming
But now I know
It was going to happen someday
I just didn't imagine so soon
And I don't know how to escape
I can't find a way out
So, tonight I'm working
On this fantastic plan
To escape this endlessness
To escape this world of pain and regret
To find myself within this hole
Tonight's the night
I find my way out of myself
And live

Top of the World

I feel on top of the world and I'm
thinking how dangerous
it would be
if I fell
because just one touch
could send me off the edge
of this platform
called love

Truth Beyond

Love met truth, truth to get denied
Life to find the one, life to realize
Risk found adventure, heart to start beating
Lungs to find first breath, blood to be releasing
Find out true feelings, hide the obvious
Look beyond figure, looks are tedious
Trust to bond, romance to be figured
Distance to separate, closeness to trigger
Connection to Earth, counties cut the line
I got him on computer, don't blame me for trying
Each moment of heartbeat, pass time by crying
Opened your eyes never, stop! My heart's denying

Two Black Roses

I'm alive, alone, by myself, no one else
On the table, I'm staring at the cards I've been dealt
No friends around, no release, no room to breathe
Two black roses, my friends gave to me
A long away, a close goodbye
A simple thought as I cry tonight
One thought, two thoughts
One life . . . gone
Broken heart, demented mind, tortured soul
A pathetic life has taken its toll
Cries for help, silent as night
Obvious as light, noticed tonight
Only cuz it's one I die
Dead alone, by myself no one else
I've thrown away the cards I've been dealt
No friends no more, no breath at all
My cries for help, dead as me
Lying next to two roses a friend gave to me

Uncovered Heart

My pain begins too soon to heal
The secrets I've hid begin to reveal
My image is modest, I'm not a slut
I'm scarred for life, I can't find a way
Can't get help, there's nothing to say
I swallow the pills, rid the pain
The blood soaks through, leaves a stain
My reason for life is to have kids
But I'm scared, look at what he did
I told him no, but I was no match
He damaged me, I felt like trash
I was scared to get into trouble
He abused me, used me, permanently bruised me, always accused me
Of doing something wrong
I was never innocent, never pure
He took my life and my glory
Depressed, stressed, overly obsessed, too young to be pressed
Into doing these things, too young to be caressed
So, if I look sad, I probably feel bad, I never knew my dad
It makes me mad
He disappeared when I was an embryo
But that made me, my twin, and my mom a tiny trio

Vague

Everything seems so unimportant
When I'm sitting next to you
And every feeling escapes me
But yet I don't know what to do

Everything is so unimportant
Even when you're away
I can't seem to be myself
I can't seem to concentrate

Everything is so unimportant
Even the biggest things
I don't know what to say to you
But you still answer the ring

And I know a text isn't much
But right now it's the most to me
And I know life can be rough
But with you, it's okay to just be

Okay to be you
Okay to be me
Okay to let you know
That in you, I believe

Weakness

Tears are my weakness
I shall not cry
Cuz if I shall start
I surely will die

Food is my weakness
I shall not crave
Cuz if I shall eat
I might as well dig my grave

Love is my weakness
I shall not desire
Cuz if I shall feel
I shall have no power

Weathered

Sparkling snowflakes, falling alone
Missing stars, the ones that don't show
Harsh rain going where the wind blows
Empty clouds, pulled away and pulled slow
I'm the sparkling snowflakes
I fell for you alone
You are the missing stars
In person is where you don't show
Life is the harsh rain
Taking me away
My heart is the empty clouds
Left with no tears, no home, no way

What I

You control my feelings, day and night
And I hate for it, I wish you'd die
And even though you're my enemy
I miss you and I wish you didn't leave

I miss your hugs to my heart and your words to my ears
And I miss how your touch almost brought me to tears
And I miss how you grabbed me to find out the truth
But I don't know if you'd tell me (the truth) if I did that to you

And I hate how you've been where I am
Because you're so far away, but you understand
And I love how you're gone, nowhere near me
So then I have to test my strength

But I hate how I told you how I felt
And I wish I hadn't told you the way that I dealt
I don't know if you caught on to my ways
But I think you know why I did it on those hard days

I hate how I'm stuck loving you
Because I'm still and you move
But I love how you're still alive
Because if you weren't, I'd die

And I hate how I'm afraid to call you
My heart will get broken if you're in a bad mood
Because the last time you told me the truth
It made me sick, sad, and I cried for you

I thought I loved you, what I would need
But truly I can't, my heart will slowly bleed
And I can't stand how I give myself away
Telling you how I feel with every breath a word to say

When I barely even knew you, you were my friend
But now that I do I feel I should end
Life goes on, true friends stay
But now I am wondering
Should I stay
Away

What I Don't Know

There's so many reconsiderations
You're just one of them
And I'm sorry I'm making this difficult
It's just that I'm scared and confused
So please be patient with me
Slowly the truth will come out

What You Make of It

The sun is slowly rising from the depths of the horizon
The beauty sweeps across as well
Nothing is moving nor making noise
It's like the day when Lucifer fell

So now I'm gazing into the sky
Asking questions to things unanswered
But I get lost too often
And I'm left without a single answer

Faintly the whispers of the wind
Blows across a valley somewhere
And a volcano erupts violently
In a place not yet discovered

Things we have no control over
Things we like to think we can predict
Things that so many of us fear
Things that are natural and we can't prevent

When I Sleep

I went to bed to fall asleep before I could think of you
But when I slept you were the only thing I saw
That's what you do to me

And in that restless dreaminess
You were the shady figure
But instead of chasing me with a knife
I was chasing you with my heart

It's like that now, in this blurry reality
I chose your heart and you ran from me
So much miscommunication
So much distress, darkness
So much I wish I could hear, the things I'm deaf to

And I should try to forget about you and yourself
But that's harder than it seems, you're still you, I'm still me
And I liked you for you, not for anybody else
And I suppose you'll still be a part of all my dreams

So hard it is to forget when you appear while I'm sleeping
And I'm curious as to when that'll end
I just hope one day soon that in my dreams, you'll stop running

Which Would You Rather Be: The Rock or The Rose

The rose
Growing into a stunning flower
Symbolizing love and beauty
Standing tall under the gleaming sun
The rose

The rock
Moving from place to place
Symbolizing reliability and protection
Strength and solidity
The rock

The rose
Showing joy and hope
Permeating smells of dark stormy nights and wondrous sunny days
All at the same time
The rose

The rock
Being rolled and thrown and moved each day
Becoming smaller and smaller or becoming parts of other rocks
Leaving itself in places, new and old
The rock

The rose
With its petals floating lifelessly over calm waters
With its stem cut rather violently and put in a glass vase in the kitchen
window
With its rarity in abundance
The rose

The rock
With its repetitive individuality
With its body as a mountain and its baby as pebbles
With its rare colors caused by selfish reactions of nature
The rock

The rose
Decaying in the darkness
Falling apart in the blustery winds of November
Browning and wrinkling from old age
The rose

The rock
Cool in the night moon, hot in the afternoon sun
Traveling all over in the blustery winds of November
Color after color, caused by Mother Nature's selfishness
The rock

The rock or the rose . . .
Which would you like to be?

With or Without

With him I have great self esteem
Without him I hate myself and how I seem
With him my face glows and I smile
Without him I get depressed for a while
With him I daydream and my thoughts wander
Without him I sit and he becomes my mind's slumber
With him I have someone to live for
Without him I'm nobody, I lock my door
With him I see the wonders of life
Without him all I want to do is cry
With him the whole world understands
Without him understanding is what no one can

Without You

These pictures are all I have left of you
They remind me of days past
Death overcame your being
And now this pain will last

You were always so beautiful
You didn't need to impress
And you always made me smile
I just won't smile anymore, I guess

You left me alone in this world
It's so lonely without you
And silence slips by slowly, sorely
And even now I feel blue

As the snow drifts by and your body's underneath
I know you're on top of this all
And I know when I die
It'd be for you, that I let time tick

(RIP my reason, the best thing that ever happened to me
Rajah K. Hill)

Women of Sin and
Lack of Peace of Mind

The light is being shown on her sins
All the abusive lies being recovered
Kneeling before the Lord, instead of all her friends
All the false hatred being discovered
The necklace hanging over her chest
She needs to see what is best
The Lord took her daughter to the heavens above
But taking the new life inside her wasn't enough
He took all her clothes except one piece
The moon and the stars giving strength to those
The healing begins but no one shall pass through
To heaven, to hell, who would have knew
She died by lack of piece of mind
That was enough to kill off her kind

Wondered

I've always wondered how thoughts work
Cuz this is so outrageous
Your stuck in my mind day and night
The picture in my mind vivacious

I close my eyes to erase your face
But I still see the outline
It's no fair how much you haunt me
All that can delete it is time

Won't

silence fills the room
except for the faint humming of music playing
on a forgotten CD player

tears stuck somewhere
I don't know where, but I know they're there
I just can't find them

I want to cry, to scream
but nothing comes to me in my emptiness
so I sit quietly, alone

I want to go on
get past my phase of sadness, depression
but it stays

I want to forget
about my old life, friends, happiness
but I can't

I want this feeling to GO AWAY
leave me alone
but it stalks me
I'm loneliness' favorite obsession

it tears me to pieces
makes my blood turn to ice
running through my veins

like the first snow
falling, falling
melting, freezing, gone, release

Worthless Words

Dark face, silent eyes, missing goodbyes
No words for open ears, communication disappears
Tragic associations, forgotten obligations
Piercing hearts, unimaginable thoughts
Blank mind, mindless actions, opposite attraction
Death wish, last breath, one request
You to know, I said, I love you

You and Me

As these days pass, I steadily think of you
How you are the one I need
How you are my first true love
How you are my piece of mind
How you're my sanity

And as we spend our time together
It makes me think of spending our lives with each other
And everything you do makes me feel good
You are my godsent painkiller
My saint, my sinner

And whatever you ask for me is for my own good
Thinking of us, not just you, not just me
And one day in our future, we may end
We may grow up holding hands, getting married
We may stay friends watching sappy movies
Getting popcorn stuck in our dentures

But whatever happens, I will love you
XOXO

You Are My Suicide

These pills I took a minute ago took every emotion I had and threw
them away
And now I'm just calm and sleepy
And I feel lonely in a good way
Because I can't think of you when you're with me

You are all that's ever on my mind
And nothing so far has changed that
And if my superpower was time rewind
To you I would go back

So one after another I empty this bottle
Each pill different, accumulated after a while
As my skin crawls and begins to get itchy
And as my eyes close, I see suicide is still an ending

As long as no one finds me, I promise I'll be okay
Because I'm thinking of you constantly, always
I try hard to forget who I'm leaving behind
But your face is still behind my closing eyes

This really wasn't my choice, you see
God was on my side
I prayed for you to believe
But you stood in vain every night

I hope you see something new
Before my heart stops beating
I love you like the Lord does
And I think you might die peacefully while bleeding

You Don't Care

I miss you and you don't care
And when I want you to write to me
You don't, you don't even care
I want to cry, to spill out my liquid tears
To share with you my many fears
But you don't care
I want to know how to reach out
Take your hand into mine
And you don't reach, you don't hold, you don't care
You may be scared
But I don't care
I just want to see your eyes, hold your hand, and for you
I'll be there

Youth and Youth Alone

And there she sat
Alone and scared
She was eighteen
Surrounded by
The world of grownups
A world she would soon
Know intimately
The trains were fast
Speeding by, leaving the
Wind as a reminder of
Its passing
And just as soon, it's
Gone
Like life
A new life inside now
A child made within herself
She had nowhere to go
Except where the train would
Take her
So, alone and scared
There she sat